SPIRITS
IN THE
SKY

SP

RITS
IN THE
SKY

The Airplanes of World War II

Photographs from the Collection of the Confederate Air Force

Foreword by Ross Perot, Jr.

Photo Editor / John Matthews   Text / Nancy Robinson Masters

Taylor Publishing Company   Dallas, Texas

The editor and author wish to express sincere appreciation to Bill Masters, Technical Advisor, and Larry C. Sanders, Chief Photographer, for their assistance in making this book possible.

Published by Taylor Publishing Company
              1550 West Mockingbird Lane
              Dallas, Texas 75235

Designed by SMITHERMANS

Library of Congress Cataloging-in-Publication Data

Spirits in the sky: the airplanes of World War Two: from the collection of the Confederate Air Force /
    photography editor, John Matthews; text by Nancy Robinson Masters.
      p. cm.
    ISBN 0-87833-724-5: $39.95
    I. Airplanes, Military—United States—History—Pictorial works.
    2. World War, 1939-1945—Equipment and supplies—Pictorial works.
    3. World War, 1939-1945—Aerial operations, American—Pictorial works.
    4. Confederate Air Force—Pictorial works.
    I. Matthews, John R., 1937-
    II. Robinson Masters, Nancy.
    III. Confederate Air Force.
    UG1243.S65 1990
    940.54'4973—dc20
                   90-34643
                   CIP

Printed in the United States of America

10 9 8 7 6 5 4 3 2 1

Overleaf: The Douglas B-26.

FOREWORD

As a lifelong aviation enthusiast and a member of the United States Air Force Reserve, I've always admired the dedication of the Confederate Air Force.

The efforts of the Confederate Air Force Ghost Squadron—to preserve, in flying condition, the combat aircraft of World War II—bring to life the indomitable spirit of the brave men and women who took part in that terrible conflict. More than just salvaging old aircraft, the CAF is keeping alive the memory of the resourcefulness, ingenuity, and courage of a nation galvanized in defense of liberty.

Finally, their work helps us remember the lessons America learned from the Second World War: lessons about preparedness, about national purpose, and about values worth fighting and dying for. These are lessons that we as Americans cannot afford to forget.

Spirits In The Sky, in keeping with this mission, conveys the majesty of the proud aircraft of the Confederate Air Force Ghost Squadron.

Ross Perot, Jr.

*A wise nation will disarm slowly.
It will continue,
long after the blood has dried on the battlefields,
to train skilled workmen in the factories,
to train young flyers and drill young soldiers,
and maintain a military might
that will assure it still as an uninviting target
for ambitious attack.*

*… The snake under the heel
must be kept under heel,
lest he come to life again at sunrise.*

General H. H. "Hap" Arnold
Chief of the U.S. Army Air Corps
September 1940

On September 1, 1939, a year before General Arnold penned this solemn warning, the German Junkers 87 Stuka dive bomber had, with screaming surprise, rained unrelenting terror on Poland.

Just over a year later on December 7, 1941, it would be the Japanese in their A6M2 Zeros who would do the same over Pearl Harbor.

On December 8, 1941, it was official:

The United States of America was at war.

Unlike any war before, this war would have to be won in the air as well as on land and sea if it was to be won at all.

Arnold was adamant in his plea for support of air power:

"The air forces which protect the Western world will have 'U.S.' painted under their metal wings."

Hap Arnold was the first airman to achieve the rank of general, and he was one of the nation's few military pilots with a flying career dating back

(overleaf) A B-25 waits its turn behind a B-24 and a B-29 in a parade of CAF bombers.

Grumman TBM torpedo bombers were used heavily in the South Pacific. After the war many were converted to forestry fire bombers.

before World War I. In 1911 he had been assigned to the Signal Corps. Six months after he presented this paper outlining to the American people the importance of air power, he was appointed Chief of the Army Air Corps and in March 1942 he became Commanding General of the Army Air Corps.

"It is unavailing if a few men perceive the correct principles of strategy and go about a nation thundering them in vain," Arnold insisted. "Adequate air power cannot be created after the necessity for it has arisen!"

In contrast to the woefully unprepared United States, Japan had nearly 3,000 and Germany had 4,100 modern, combat-ready aircraft.

Prodded by Arnold, American industrial leaders working in the competitive free-enterprise system already had on the drawing boards most of the planes that would become America's "Air Armada," but mass aircraft production was still unknown.

In the thirty-two years from the time the Wright brothers began building aircraft to 1940, U.S. companies had produced a total of only 75,000 planes.

P-63, gear up and climbing.

By the war's end a rejuvenated American manufacturing industry had actually delivered 296,431 aircraft.

At peak production this was one plane every six minutes.

With that same deadly deliberation and efficiency, the United States of America destroyed, one by one, the magnificent planes of war it had created.

This book is not the story of what happened to all those airplanes. Nor is it intended to be a complete pictorial record of all the aircraft represented in General Arnold's "legion marked 'U.S.'."

This book is simply visual testimony to what every pilot and every crew member knew—but could not explain—to those who never felt the surging rhythm of a round engine or smelled the oily smoke of exhaust stacks.

These airplanes were more than mere metal and magnetos.

This is a book about airplanes that did not die.

It is the story of spirits that could not be crushed or melted no matter how forgotten the battle . . .

No matter how hot the fire.

The P-26 was one of the last open-cockpit Boeings built. It was based in China against the Japanese and flew in the Phillipine Air Force.

The L-4 wearing the invasion stripes of June 6, 1944. Easily recognizable as the J-3 Cub, the L-4 was one of several liaison aircraft that played a major role in the air war.

(overleaf) A privately owned PBY was flown as part of the worldwide commemoration of the 75th anniversary of naval aviation.

(above) A civilian conversion of the PBY Navy patrol bomber.
The PBY was already in manufacture at the beginning of the
war and saw duty as the OA-10 for the Air Corps.

(right) The blister on a PBY-5A Navy
plane was used for surveillance.

The Stearman PT-17 trainer.

The CAF's SNJ-4 sponsored by the Big Country Squadron is the Navy version of the T-6 Texan. Both were used as advance trainers.

An ME 109 in desert camouflage, Africa, 1942.

(overleaf) The Douglas DC-3 became the Army Air Corps' C-47. DC-3s
are still in service around the world, but few wear invasion markings.

The Bearcat was built to replace the Hellcat, but never saw combat in WWII.

A Pratt & Whitney 1340 engine powers the SNJ-4 N6411D
Big Country One.

*Due to the value of the
military airplane and all its parts,
it is important that nothing be thrown away…
Wherever possible
a wrecked or damaged plane is repaired
and put back in the air again.*

Official Army Air Corps Guide, 1944

To some it is ugly and grotesque.
The glory that was once an F6F-3 Hellcat is now just a pathetic rotted skeleton anchored to the dry Sonoran Desert sand in southern Arizona at the Pima Air Museum outdoor display. Once, flattops on rolling seas were the only homes these 42-foot wings knew; then, salt water, not sand, sprayed the open cockpit.

Beginning in 1943, Hellcat pilot and carrier power wrought death and destruction for 4,947 Japanese aircraft in air-to-air combat. The Hellcat accounted for almost eighty percent of the aircraft Navy pilots destroyed in the skies, with another 209 of the Rising Sun's air force crushed on the ground by the Grumman-built fighter.

Larger and more powerful than the older Grumman Wildcat, the Hellcat was the first carrier-based airplane in the Pacific to do what no other

This Grumman Hellcat recovered from the ocean was beyond restoration. When it was discovered that its gun would still fire, aircraft scrap dealers joked that the old plane was haunted, and it was allowed to be displayed at Pima Air Museum rather than sent to the smelters.

American fighter could do: turn inside the Japanese Zero.

But not this one. In 1944, twelve miles off the coast of San Diego, its engine quit. The pilot bailed out but the plane sank. For twenty-six years the Hellcat rested at the bottom of the ocean before being dredged up, a rotted remain of another era.

Ironically, it was the ocean rot that spared this Hellcat the fate of the white-hot scrap smelters just down the road from Pima—where 25,000 bombers, fighters, and other World War II aircraft were actually flown from wartime fame into smelter fires.

At the end of the war, four billion dollars of surplus aircraft was sold as scrap by the War Assets Administration for $6.5 million. Two hundred million pounds of reusable aluminum alloy was reclaimed and recycled into metal for America's postwar population boom. Gear doors became gutters. Fuselages became dinner forks. Wings that bore the letters "U.S." became urinals and were exported to countries once loyal to the Axis powers.

Pilots leaning across an F6F on board the USS Lexington *after shooting down 17 out of 20 Japanese planes heading for Tarawa.*

It was decided that this Hellcat pulled from the ocean would be studied for the effects of corrosion and then put on display without restoration. That it was spared the ignoble death so many of its brothers had suffered may be attributed to a discovery made by its underwater rescuers:

> After being submerged twenty-six years, the inboard gun on
> the port wing fired with no mechanical difficulties!

Some say that scrap dealers refused to bargain for the haunted hulk. Others say there wasn't enough salvage left to make it worthwhile.

Back in the late 1950s, some farmers and crop dusters from the Texas Rio Grande Valley had been having considerable fun flying their war surplus P-51 Mustang.

Unaware that World War II aircraft were dying by the thousands in disposal depots, the group had loosely banded together under the name

Fighters past and present.... A modern F-15 climbs behind a P-51.

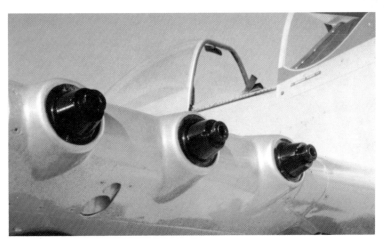

Three of a P-51's six .50-caliber guns.

Confederate Air Force, and much to their surprise found themselves sought after to fly the Mustang at air shows and aviation displays. Despite the new jet-age technology, people still wanted to see planes with pistons that drank oil and propellers that split eardrums.

For the grand sum of $2,500, duster pilot Lloyd Nolen, along with Bill Turnbull, Billy Drawe, Royce Norman, and C.W. Butler—some of them ex-service pilots, some just aviation enthusiasts—had acquired one of the first Mustangs released from Korean War service. For Nolen it was sweet revenge. As an Army Air Corps instructor in World War II, he had trained

(overleaf) George Preddy, John C. Meyer, and Don Gentile became "aces" in Merlin-powered P-51 Mustangs with 25, 24, and 23 victories respectively. After WWII a P-51 could be purchased for as little as $1,500.

Navy crewmen aboard the USS Monterey *bringing an F6F to the flight deck on an elevator.*

countless student pilots, but he had never got to fly the fighters they went on to command.

Nolen promised himself he'd have his own fighter someday, the Army Air Corps be damned.

In 1951 he had made good on that promise. A P-40 Warhawk in need of hoses, radiators, and protection from the scrap heap found a home in Mercedes, Texas, at the duster pilot's strip. Nolen soon sold the P-40 in anticipation of buying a Mustang, but in 1952 the P-51s were recalled to combat in Korea. Not until a few years later, in 1957, were the fighters again released for civilian purchase... or for scrap.

It seemed foolish in a way. Twenty-five hundred dollars was hard money for a duster pilot and his friends to come by in the fifties after a drought, and you sure couldn't dogfight a field of lettuce.

But they bought the Mustang anyway.

No one claims responsibility for painting "Confederate Air Force" on the

F4F Wildcats in formation over the Pacific.

Mustang's fuselage under the stabilizer. It just appeared there one Sunday morning. But it seemed to fit the mood of the men who refused to be bothered by the whispers and stares of people who didn't understand what pleasure they derived from flying the old Mustang.

Still, you couldn't have an air force without at least two airplanes, the group decided, and they began to search for another fighter to complement the Mustang.

Soon it was 1959. World War II was a fading memory to most Americans. What Nolen and the others were soon to discover about the destruction of that war's planes had been happening since 1945 and would inspire a movement by the thousands of men and women who had built, flown, and maintained the nearly 300,000 U.S. airplanes that secured the world's skies in history's darkest hours.

They learned that thirty-two F8F Bearcats were to be auctioned at Litchfield Park Naval Air Station near Phoenix, Arizona. Nolen and Turnbull

(left) The C-46 Commando.

33

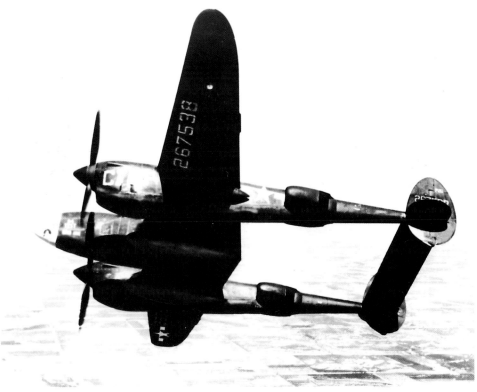

The Japanese called it the "fork-tailed devil," but the P-38 made a believer out of any who doubted its abilities when it shot down a Japanese bomber carrying Admiral Yamamoto.

The P-38 readies for takeoff.

A gaggle of T-6s and SNJs fly formation once more for airshow crowds at Breckenridge, Texas.

bought two at a bargain-basement price of $805 each.

The Bearcat was Grumman's last production piston-engined fighter. The war had ended without the Bearcat ever seeing combat. Like the Hellcat, the Bearcat was built for the Navy. But it was smaller than the Hellcat and much lighter. After the war, Navy squadrons had continued to be re-equipped with the Bearcat, but by 1952 the planes were taken out of active service. Most of the fighters were sold to the French and the Royal Thai air forces.

That a bunch of farmers and duster pilots in the Texas Valley would want to buy an F8F Bearcat to fly with a P-51 Mustang just for fun seemed ludicrous, especially since the two F8Fs they had bid for were in deplorable condition. It took the men six weeks working in the scorching desert sun to make the two airplanes even flyable. The other thirty F8Fs, it was learned, were to be melted into fat square ingots in the Arizona smelters.

Through the weeks and months that followed, the realization that the

The Grumman Wildcat, like every radial-engine airplane, required a continual supply of oil for its cylinders. Posters encouraging "An oil well for each engine" were inspiration for American petroleum producers during WWII.

overwhelming bulk of America's mighty war planes were being systematically done away with moved this group to anger—anger that an important part of their past was being destroyed. That anger moved them to action.

The extent of the destruction was frightening. There wasn't a single flying P-47 "Jug" left of the 15,000 built. Only a handful of Corsairs and Lightnings remained. The TBMs, B-26s, and B-17s had been sliced, smashed, chunked, and crushed with absolutely no effort from the military services or the government to keep at least one of each in flying condition.

With a growing sense of panic that they might be too late, the small band of believers combed the disposal depots and talked with crane operators who described the piece-by-piece destruction of Airacobras, Torpedo Bombers, and Mitchells. Whether liaison L-Birds or B-24 Liberators, the stories didn't change.

"We watched part of a B-17 pushed into hell," CAF co-founder Lefty Gardner reported after visiting the scrap yards. "It made us all too sick to

A single .50-caliber gun from the TBM torpedo bomber gunner's turret was a deadly force to be reckoned with. The half-inch shell was devastatingly destructive at more than a quarter mile.

eat, so we drank whiskey for two days and swore we'd save every one we could." With these few words Gardner had unknowingly outlined the mission for the Confederate Air Force. These men sensed that a nation that would destroy its wartime aircraft relics could someday forget the lessons the war had taught at such great cost.

In the summer of 1961, the first Official Confederate Air Force Statement of Policy was published. In part, this was what it reported:

"A group of pilots went out to see what was left at the surplus disposal depots in the Arizona Territory. What they saw made these men sad, and then made them angry. They were chopping up and smelting down good airplanes by the hundreds! The T-6, C-45, F8F, F4U, TBM, B-25, B-26, and many others were on the block. The older types had long since been completely destroyed.

"On checking into this revolting situation, it was found that

The Bell P-63 Kingcobra was the successor to the underpowered P-39.

The AD-1 Skyraider was another WWII design that did not see actual service until the war was over. Modern electronic technology has brought about significant changes in its instrument panel, once considered among the most advanced.

The Fleet, with its single-row Kinner radial engines, was used as a trainer in the early days of WWII.

Workmen spin the propellor of a finished FV-1 at the Vega Aircraft plant at Burbank, California.

The Stinson L-5 was one of thousands of liaison aircraft used as trainers, artillery spotters, personnel transports, and for dozens of other duties by the Army Air Corps.

Bullseyes, checkerboards, and stars were commonly painted on the dustcovers of BT-13 wheels. While regulations determined what could be painted, the design was usually left to the imagination of the maintenance crew.

The glossy new paint on a T-6 reflects the early
football-shaped ADF antenna housing. A number
of WWII aircraft were so equipped.

This BT-13A trainer was commissioned exactly one month before the
bombing of Pearl Harbor. The well-worn wooden control stick is a typical
example of the use of wood to conserve metal in aircraft construction.

Tails of BT-13s, AT-6s, and SNJs painted with Japanese markings comprised the "Tora! Tora!
Tora!" group used in the CAF re-creation of the December 7, 1941 bombing of Pearl Harbor.

in the future no combat-type aircraft would be sold for flying or display purposes. They were to be destroyed. No attempt was being made to ensure at least one was left in flying condition for future generations to see.

"We cannot let America totally destroy these airplanes which helped to win a world war. We cannot let America forget."

The end.

The beginning.

The goal was simple and clear: to acquire at least one of each type of fighter aircraft and maintain them in flying, fighting trim.

The price would be high. There were no funds outside their own pockets. The rewards would be mostly intangible and ephemeral, like the dust of a tail-wheel landing that appears for an instant and then disappears forever.

Men named Bates, Ellis, Southwick, Wells, Downing, Jones, and Wallace—veterans, friends, pilots, or just supporters—signed on with Nolen and Gardner, promising to tackle every task necessary to reach the goal... everything, that is, except leading the singing for the meetings. "Our singing needs considerable improvement. We will have to appoint a volunteer to lead the singing at the next meeting," the March 3, 1961, newsletter stated. Someone had to have a sense of humor with such a grim task ahead.

History has failed to record who got the first song leader's job.

In 1961 the Confederate Air Force was officially granted a charter by the State of Texas. The doubters were still shaking their heads, but believers from across the country began joining to support the "Rebels'" cause. Others who did not join were still inspired to collect and restore to original flying condition these "spirits in the sky."

By the end of 1961, the CAF fleet had grown from two to nine aircraft. In addition to the Mustang and the Bearcat, there was one FM-2 Wildcat, one F6F Hellcat, one FG1D Corsair, one P-38 Lightning, one P-40 Warhawk, one B-25 Mitchell, and three AT-6 Texans.

Just thirty years after America had been caught sleeping at Pearl Harbor, a handful of men with a few forgotten planes had awakened another sleeping giant.

Resolve... Resurrection... Restoration. The movement had begun.

But how do you resurrect cold metal cowlings and silent propellers?

How do you restore the magic of 2,000 horsepower surging through a radial engine to a single throttle held in the grip of a pilot's hand?

The answers, like the varieties of aircraft, are legion.

The Bell P-39 Airacobra was first flown in 1939. It featured a nosewheel-type landing gear and the engine behind the pilot. 9,588 were built.

A rare PT-23 trainer.

(above) A privately owned PBY.
(below) The CG-4A assault glider was also known as the British Hadrian. It could carry up to 15 fully armed troops. Although 12,393 were built, none are still flying. The CG-4A was built to be expendable.

As each phoenix rises from the ashes to fly, each World War II aircraft restoration is a unique story. And the Confederate Air Force is not alone in this endeavor. Hundreds of individuals, corporations, communities, and organizations joined to preserve the craft of World War II, and not just as silent static displays.

The airplanes must fly.

Each restoration is a commitment to the legacy of aviation's historic treasures.

This privately owned BT-13 basic trainer is typical of the WWII aircraft that have been restored to flying condition. Prices range from $40,000 and up

Left tire shredded and the oleo punctured.
No. 3 engine lost prop and 2 bottom cylinders.
Hole in the left tank, flux-gate compass blown out,
bomb bay doors and belly turret gone.

Gee, I sure hope they get that compass fixed
before we have to fly again.

B-17 Bombardier's log, 1944

Frank Gates Gardner
became the first licensed airframe and power plant (A&P) mechanic in
1927, the same year Charles Lindbergh made history as the first pilot to
fly solo across the Atlantic.

Lindbergh's name became a household word.

Gardner's did not.

Thus it seemed destined for those who built and maintained the mighty
machines of war to be always overshadowed by the pilots who pushed
the throttles.

Between Pearl Harbor and the end of the war, 695,866 aircraft mechanics
were trained by the Army Air Corps.

The mechanics' hands were perpetually greasy, scratched, and scarred
from nursing massive radial engines. No amount of soap and gasoline could
remove the grimy evidence of their trade from beneath their fingernails.
Their fingers were strong enough to hold steel tubing in place, yet gentle

enough to stretch a piece of sheer cotton fabric across the same steel without a snag or tear.

Mechanics had to rely on their senses of touch, feel, and even taste to tell them what they needed to know. Proper tools and equipment were often scarce or nonexistent in the aircraft-staging areas of the theaters of war.

"Noise abatement" to mechanics working in unheated wooden hangars was seldom more than cotton in the ears. Hand protection meant wearing whatever size pair of gloves you were issued.

There were two unwritten rules among the aircrews: rule number one, Never trust a mechanic who isn't hard of hearing; and rule number two, Never trust a mechanic with missing fingers.

From the jungles of New Guinea to the deserts of North Africa, it was these uncelebrated mechanics who had the unending duty of keeping the planes flying for the pilots who got all the glory.

New, metal fighting planes are stouter than the flesh and blood of their crews. They can be made ready for a return engagement before their crews can be rested.

General Hap Arnold, 1940

Henry Tillett Jr. was a Navy pilot in World War I. When he could not re-enlist for World War II as a pilot because of his age, Tillett took on one of the toughest assignments to be had: supervising the aircraft sheet-metal repair shop at Pearl Harbor.

"I usually didn't sleep for two or three days at a time," remembers Tillett. "The airplanes were coming in so fast and were in such terrible condition I ordered that only one worker at a time was to sleep.

"My men hated me, but I had no choice. We had to turn 'em around, get 'em back out. It got so I could recognize some of 'em after I'd fixed 'em a dozen times. Our hope was that we'd keep getting to fix the same airplanes again because if an airplane didn't come back again for repairs, it meant a crew didn't come back."

Tillett recalled being so grateful he could cry.

"Sometimes it was all that kept me awake. I had a boy out flying those airplanes and every time I pounded the metal I was pounding the dirty dogs who were trying to kill him."

Tillett and his son both went home to Texas when the war was over—one with pilot's wings, and one with ten crooked fingers and permanently damaged eardrums.

The fuselage of a P-51 all jigged up but not ready to go. When the restoration is completed on this airplane it will be worth in excess of $500,000.

P-40 engine repairs.

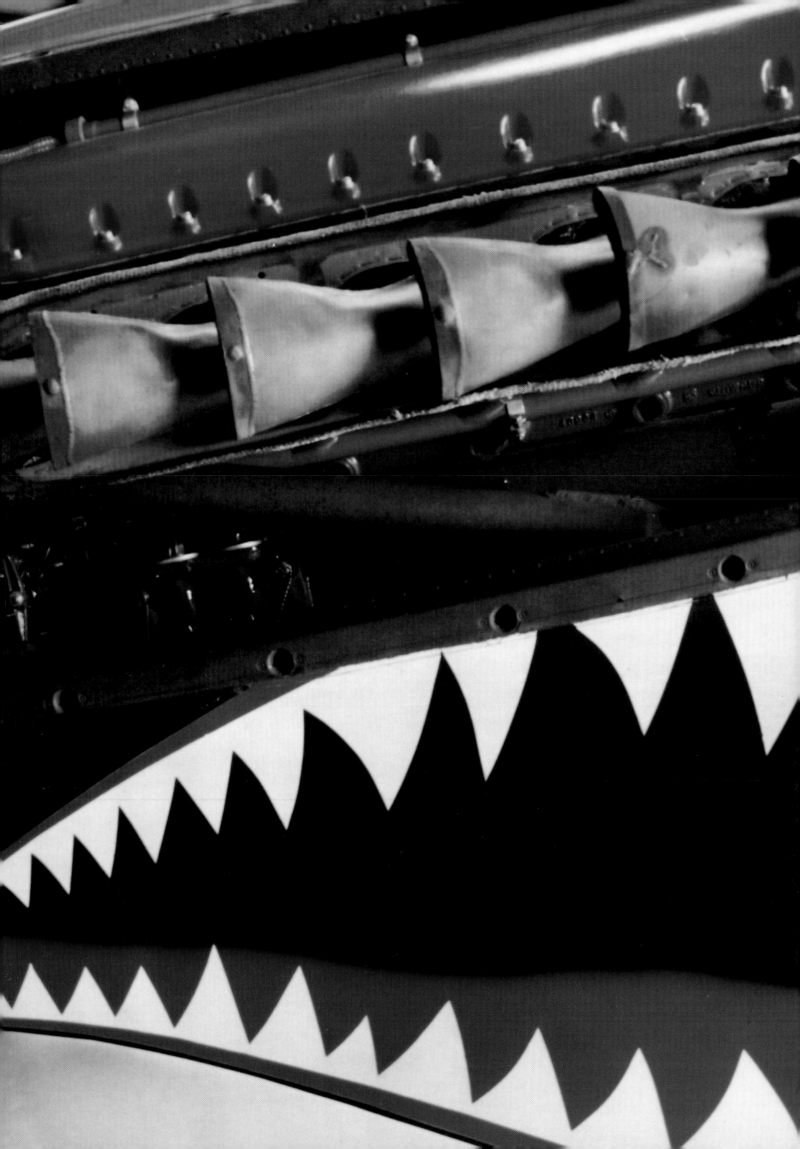

(left) The P-40 powerplant after repairs looks as good as when it was new almost five decades ago.

The P-40 air-scoop flow dividers directed intake air to cool the airplane's three different radiators.

As a result of tests in 1941, jet units to reduce normal takeoff runs as much as 60% were installed on Navy aircraft. Doubly powered by the flow of jet units, a Navy Vought Corsair fighter plane roars off the deck of an aircraft carrier on one of the first JATO (Jet Assisted Takeoff) operations September 9, 1944.

"Look at 'em, just sittin' there leakin'."

A fighter pilot's disgusted observation of the B-25 Mitchell and the A-26 Invader sitting on the flight line of Rebel Field wasn't unusual. Fighter pilots never could figure out why anyone would want to fly a bomber.

If it had more than one engine and more than one seat, a fighter pilot just wasn't interested.

The Confederate Air Force collection of all ten American fighters involved in World War II was completed in 1963. Each of the ten aircraft had been flown to CAF headquarters with the exception of the P-39, which was delivered in hundreds of small pieces by truck from Hobbs, New Mexico. Now ten craft plus sixty-six members equaled the entire Confederate Air Force.

As far as the fighter pilots were concerned, the collection was complete. But the memory of the cranes and smelters and the B-17 bombers being pasteurized into barn roofs had not been totally forgotten by the rest, whose love for airplanes superseded their personal preferences as pilots.

Talk began. Why not a collection of bombers?

Why not a B-17? A B-24? A B-26?

Hell, why not a B-29?

An F4U Corsair catches the first wire on the USS Essex *on January 1, 1945.*

The audacity of even imagining such a project sparked the discussion into a definite decision to do it. The odds of resurrecting one, much less all four, of these aircraft wouldn't have had a taker at any track.

Not only would the aircraft have to be found, paid for, and restored to flying status, but they would continue to have to be "fed, watered, and stabled" at four times the rate of the single-engine fighters.

> *The bomber must not turn and fight; his is not a fighting mission. He plows straight to the target, disdainful of bursting shells from below or lightning fighter thrusts from above. The crew will never do better work than when rocking in the tempest of antiaircraft fire or when enemy fighter bullets are tearing great chunks from their planes' metal sides.*
>
> General Hap Arnold, 1940

Lieutenant Myron Crissy and Mr. Phillip O. Parmalee demonstrated the first drop of a live bomb January 15, 1911, near San Francisco. But in 1940

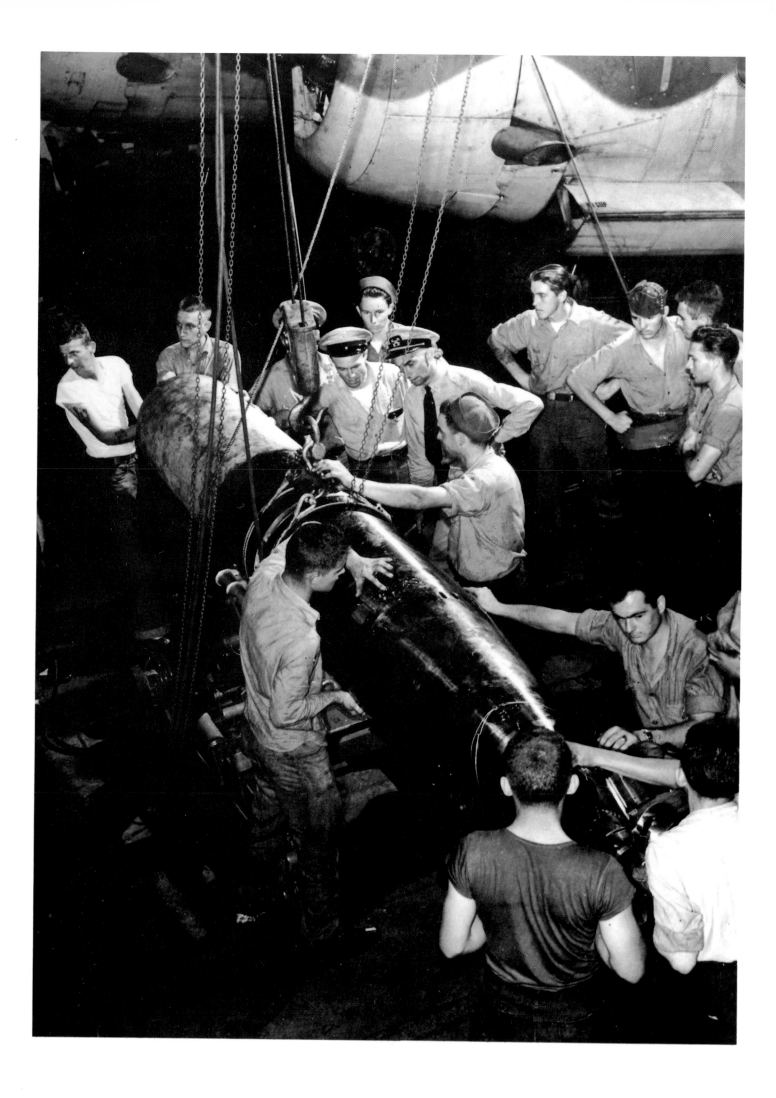

The P-43 built by Republic was the predecessor to the P-47.

Hap Arnold was still trying to convince America that dropping bombs on strategic supply sources was the way to win a war.

"The most economical way of reducing a large city to the point of surrender, of breaking its will to resistance, is not to drop bombs in its streets, but to destroy the power plants which supply light, the water supply, the sewer lines," he stated.

In May 1934 the U.S. Army Air Corps had issued a design specification for a multiengined antishipping bomber to defend the nation against enemy fleets. The result was the giant Boeing Model 299, known as the B-17, which first flew in 1935. By June 1939, when Boeing production lines were building B-17 B models with a new nose and bigger flaps and rudders, the name that had been applied to these first U.S. heavy bombers—"Flying Fortress"—meant exactly that.

As impressive as the Flying Fortresses were, some painful lessons still lay ahead.

The Royal Air Force was the first to use B-17s on high-altitude daylight

The P-47 Thunderbolt made its first "kill" on April 15, 1943, when it replaced the Spitfire against the German Fw 190. The airplane had massive firepower, but was slow to climb until later versions were equipped with the paddle-blade propeller.

TBFs aboard the USS Monterey leaving on a bombing mission over Tinian Island, the Japanese-held island nearest to Saipan.

The P-61 Black Widow night fighter used radar extensively to find its targets. It came into service in May 1941 and was first used against the Germans by the RAF.

Razorback P-47.

B-17 Flying Fortresses in formation were a common sight in WWII; today, such a sight is extremely unusual.

North American P-82 fighter-bomber escort was a two-pilot aircraft built for long range. The Twin Mustang pilots were to alternate rest times to stay in the air.

The Bell P-39 Airacobra.

(right) The B-25 Mitchell was named in honor of gutsy Army Air Corps officer Billy Mitchell, who was court-martialled in 1924 for his efforts to promote air power. Jimmy Doolittle's use of the B-25 to raid Tokyo forever assured the twin-engine bomber's place in history.

The B-17C flown by the Royal Air Force. Note the absence of tail guns. A major redesign of the B-17 was required to add this protection.

raids. They found that the Browning guns froze at high altitude and that the Germans could catch them from behind in the plane's blind spot.

The British had good reason not to like the Yanks' "Fort."

By the end of 1942, new rugged G models were in place with the U.S. Eighth Air Force. They boasted exhaust-driven turbochargers, a plexiglass nose, dorsal, ball, and tail turrets, flush staggered waist guns, and a 12,800-pound bomb-load capacity. A total of 8,680 G models were built, and for three years the shadow of the B-17's 102-foot wings swept steadily across Europe and throughout the Pacific.

In his attempts to gather support for building bombers, Arnold outlined a "typical" routine bombing mission:

"An airplane factory thought to have been destroyed months before is showing signs of operation again. It must be destroyed.

"A trained bomber flight of six planes is assigned the mission. Takeoff is set for midnight; the route is determined, the

The Arizona Wing's B-17, Sentimental Journey, was named in a contest that drew more than 800 entries from around the world. Note the chin turret with two late-model .50 caliber guns and the two guns in the nose.

B-17 tailgunners were equipped with two .50 caliber guns. The tailgunner's position was once described as "the loneliest spot in the sky until the fighting starts."

69

approach figured to avoid heaviest known concentrations of antiaircraft fire. Combat crews retire for rest, the maintenance crews continue to tune up engines.

"Midnight comes; weather at home airdrome is soupy; individual takeoff is announced, with assembly above the overcast at a predesignated altitude and over a well-known geographical landmark when visible. The flight leader moves out from the flying line to the runway. At one-minute intervals the others follow. Flight leader pulls up through the overcast at 10,000, moves by celestial navigation to prearranged rendezvous point. At 1:00 A.M. the flight is assembled in formation echeloned to the right and heads on its course. All lights are turned out except a dim running light in rear and on top of each fuselage.

"Succeeding planes in the stepped-up formation follow tiny starlike specks on the backs of the preceding gray ghosts.

"An hour later there is a brief flash of leader's wing-tip lights. All pilots see the warning and watch for the order to attack. It is clearing now; clouds are broken. Engines are throttled; there is a slow descent to optimum bombing altitude. The planes drop back and take up one-mile intervals. Gunners are vigilant at gun stations and clear for action. Soon a bright light bursts thousands of feet below; the leader has dropped a bombing flare; there below, light as day, stand the forms of factories. Immediately rocketlike bursts fill the elements. The enemy antiaircraft has gone into action.

"Then, there is a red-specked white burst far below in that hapless factory yard; number two was a little short; number three readjusts; other bursts cover the plane plant as each succeeding bomber drops its deadly cargo. The leader has moved to a predesignated assembly point at full speed; others follow, moving through the great cloud patches for cover. The last plane lags a little, as he must photograph the job, take a picture of the work of the four which bombed the target.

"Searchlights stab the night, looking frantically for the six ghostly visitors who have disappeared into the night.

"Off to the left, telltale streaks of moving light indicate that hostile fighters with engines full out have left the ground hurriedly and pulled skyward in steep climbs to hunt the slower enemy bombers.

(overleaf) Texas Raiders *readies for takeoff.*   71

Aircraft fuselages were often marked with bombs to indicate the number of missions the airplane completed. The B-17 Texas Raiders outlasted many of its crews, who were allowed to rest after a certain number of missions while the bomber kept flying.

"A hundred miles back toward home. The bombers fall in like children into a feather bed. No longer can the enemy pursuit trail the retreating explosive freighters. At 3:30 A.M. the leader, breaking through at 500 feet, comes in on a long glide and taxies to its area on a corner of the field. Others follow. Tired crews gather at Squadron Operations.

"A telephone call goes to Headquarters, 'Mission completed'."

It sounded so easy, so simple, so sure.

But it wasn't. Even then Arnold hinted of the real war the men in the bombers would face.

"Not always is there friendly cloud cover; sometimes the searchlights catch a luckless bomber. Gas tanks burst with puffs of flame; crews bail out. On more than one occasion upon returning after long hours away from the home airdrome, the fog has moved in. Then the slower process of riding the beams for blind landing is required. The crippled and limping planes, with engines out, land on any airdrome they can reach.

"The greatest protection of the bomber, once it is discovered by enemy pursuit, lies in tight formation with the resultant grouping of defensive firepower; discipline in station keeping means safety; to scatter or break formation is disastrous."

Tight formation. Grouping of defensive firepower.

Discipline in station keeping.

Hap Arnold could have been describing the people who came together twenty-four years later in one of the bigger CAF fund-raising efforts.

A B-17 had finally been found still flying in commercial agriculture service in Pennsylvania. Though it was no longer in full military configuration, the owner was willing to sell, and the price was "only" $50,000. Seventy-two people put up the money, and Lefty Gardner headed for Pennsylvania to bring the new treasure home.

"I kept thinking, 'At least this one won't end up like those others in the smelter. This one's going to live.'"

Returning the ship to combat colors and markings was the first objective. But that posed a dilemma: The B-17 had served with many units, and there was no one way to accurately depict them all in the restoration.

The CAF asked General Curtis E. LeMay to choose the markings. In his reply of March 25, 1970, General LeMay wrote:

> "I'm afraid you've given me an impossible task. If I tried to select the one airplane with the most distinguished combat record, it would be just one man's opinion.
>
> "I suggest you drop the thought of trying to depict one airplane... I think you should try to depict the one trait of the U.S. Air Force. 'NO BOMBING ATTACK WAS EVER TURNED BACK BY ENEMY ACTION.' On two occasions that I remember, entire groups were shot out of the sky but no one turned back. This happened to the 305th Group and to the 100th Group. To me, this ranks with the Alamo, Pickett's Charge, and other great fights of our history.
>
> "Since the 305th was in action longer than the 100th I would paint your B-17 with 305th markings. I looked at some old movies and an authentic tail number is 124592."

And that's exactly the way it was done.

But it wasn't until 1982 that restoration was fully begun to return *Texas Raiders* to complete combat configuration from a modified B-17 to an authentic combat-equipped G model B-17. By this time another CAF B-17 restoration project was underway in Arizona.

The Arizona CAF members stared in awe at the size of the project they were about to undertake to restore the weary warrior to its former glory.

In 1978 N9323Z was purchased for the CAF from a corporation in California that had been using the tired old bird as an air tanker. Built by

Texas Raiders *flies into the smoke at an annual CAF Air Power Demonstration airshow.*

B-17 Flying Fortress after a successful 1944 bombing run.

Douglas under a Boeing contract, this G model had been accepted by the Army Air Corps in March 1945 and had served well in the Pacific theater.

Where are aircraft such as B-17s restored?

Not just in hangars and workshops, but in backyards and barns, basements and bathtubs. In any aircraft restoration project, conflicts born of numerous choices must be resolved: whether to make the airplane pretty and flyable, or authentic and flyable.

Sometimes choice is eliminated when authentic usable parts can no longer be found or fabricated.

Aircraft restorers wanting authentic and not pretty must dig in junkyards, search known or suspected accident sites, and beg, bargain, or trade with anyone who has an item they need.

They must not be dishonest, but at the same time they must not be above trickery. They must possess the obsession of a lover and the cunning of a fox. They must know how to be diplomatic and charming, devious and determined.

Authentic aircraft restorers are born with creative minds, sticky fingers, and patience. They do not work by the clock, but by the time it takes for paint to dry or glue to set. They may forget their children's birthdays or when to change their clothes, but they never forget which cable fits which pully or the number of rivets in a tail section.

Someone else may eventually operate the controls of the airplane, but only a dedicated aircraft restorer can make the plane live again.

The early Martin B-26 Marauder had a reputation for being an airplane "only its mother could love."

The name *Sentimental Journey* had been selected for the Arizona B-17 in a newspaper contest. Though the aircraft was in excellent shape, without four operational turrets, operational bomb bays, navigator and radio operator stations, a Norden bomb sight, and machine guns, she was still not an authentic Flying Fortress.

The airplane was voluntarily grounded by those who made her into one.

Hands of all shapes and sizes and both sexes took it apart piece by piece to concentrate on five areas of restoration: paint and reskinning, wiring, radio rooms, bomb bay doors, and top ball and tail turrets.

A lot of people said it would never fly again. The risks involved in getting the pieces back together, especially losing or breaking irreplaceable parts, were high.

A lot of people were wrong.

Determined to make *Sentimental Journey* completely authentic, the restorers began their dirty work. The interior was stripped of all paint and gunk, and toothbrushes were used to clean every crack and cranny.

Skin from the nose, around the cockpit, and back to the top of the bomb bay was pulled.

Every inch of electrical wire was removed and replaced. Instrument panels, complete with lettering and artwork, and a new radio system were installed. A new radio operator's table and radio racks were positioned.

Boeing employees personally installed the new nose turret, the first major piece of equipment of the restoration.

The group had all but despaired of securing a top turret when someone happened upon one sitting atop a gas station in Oregon. It had been there for thirty-seven years but was still in good shape. The gas station owners were cooperative and agreed to donate the usable turret in exchange for a fabricated replacement dummy. That task involved the help of a bathtub manufacturer, 1,400 miles in a rental van, and forty-eight hours of hard work installing the replica, complete with a pair of simulated .50 caliber machine guns.

Through the years others had tried to bargain for that turret and failed, but it took the determination of the *Sentimental Journey* restorers to pull it off.

And, just as the turret was about to leave for Arizona, the station owners got a call from Texas. The *Texas Raiders* restoration project was in need of a top turret. Any chance of making a deal?

The competition between the two B-17 projects, while frequently downplayed and always subtle, was nonetheless an inspiration factor for both restoration projects. For the *Texas Raiders* restoration, the most extensive single problem was corrosion control from nose to tail. The A-1 top turret was finally replaced with a new model, but instead of coming from the top of a gas station, this one came from the Eighth Air Force Museum.

And the Arizona B-17 that was predicted never to fly again?

It missed by just fourteen days its original target date of being airborne.

One of *Texas Raiders'* first appearances after a winter of concentrated restoration was in conjunction with a visit by General LeMay to CAF headquarters. When he finished touring the restored Flying Fortress, he said exactly what everyone who had scraped, primed, painted, wired, twisted, scrounged, and polished wanted to hear:

"Hell, we didn't have anything this good in Europe."

"Without the B-17," said General Carl Spaatz, first Air Force Chief of Staff, soon after victory had been achieved, "we might have lost the war."

And just thirty years later, an unbiased CAF observer put it simply: "Without authentically restored bombers, the only old airplanes we'd still have flying would be a bunch of leaking single-engine fighters."

Silent belts of .50-caliber ammunition, which was used in many U.S. aircraft in WWII.

Two very pretty young women
wearing good-looking dress uniforms, but with no gold bars,
would come to the enlisted men's mess hall for supper.
They were girls from Avenger Field, Texas,
ferrying B-26 planes in and out of Dodge City
and other B-26 bases.

We learned to watch for them
as they flew the plane out.
They used a little more than half of the runway,
stuck the nose of the plane up at a steep angle,
and went on about their business.

Most of the men used all of the runway
and hoped they got the wheels up
in time to clear the boundary fence.
Two of them that I knew of
didn't make it over the fence.
I never thought that those girls from Avenger Field
were ever given the credit that they deserved.

Jack Rowell, retired Army Air Corps instructor

Of the 19,614 medium and light bombers acquired by the Army Air Force between July 1940 and August 1945, there were 8,479 lost: 5,225 overseas, 3,254 in the United States.

During the war, Americans understood the loss of aircraft and crews in battle. It was a simple fact of war to be expected. But losses in testing,

Devil Dog is a PBJ, the Navy version of the B-25.

A beautifully restored B-25.

training, and transportation on the home front, where no enemy bullets were being fired, were somehow harder to accept.

Yet those who died in the wheat fields of Kansas gave just as much as those who died in *Der Grosse Schlag*—the big aerial blow launched by the Axis powers in 1944 to enable the *Luftwaffe* to regain control of the sky.

Der Grosse Schlag failed. Allied bombing attacks had so severely destroyed German railroads and fuel supplies that German pilots had to skimp on vital navigational training. That kept them from launching the 2,500 fighters that were supposed to saturate the American fighter escort in the winter of 1944.

On New Year's Day, 1945, the *Luftwaffe* attempted a desperate move. Risking their last reserves of fuel, its commanders ordered an attack on Allied airfields. They struck hard, destroying 127 Allied aircraft on the ground and damaging 133. But the price was high: in return they lost about 200 aircraft to flak and fighters, much more than they could afford.

"It was the Allied aircraft that kept the war in our own country and doomed us to defeat," stated Dr. Albert Speer, Germany's Reichminister for Armaments and War Production.

The Douglas B-18 bomber was in service in Hawaii in the early days of the war.

By the time the war in the Pacific ended with the Japanese surrender on August 14, 1945, more than eight thousand American medium bombers were still intact at home and abroad. Among the survivors were an impressive number of the airplanes that "divided the men from the boys," or as Jack Rowell remembers, "the girls from the men."

It was the B-26 Martin Marauder, a sleek, graceful machine, that was ordered right off Martin Aircraft designer Peyton Magruder's drawing board and into the air without benefit of prototype or testing.

To say it was initially unpopular with those who didn't truly understand its unique wing design and flight characteristics would be putting it mildly.

The uninitiated pilots called it a "widow maker" and dubbed it "the airplane even its mother had to learn to love."

Those who understood the highly streamlined advanced design, like tailgunner Denny McFarland, were disgusted with "those damn pilots who don't know how to do anything except push up the power and wait for the airplane to do the rest.

"You could be doing 200 screaming down the runway and never get off the ground unless you got the nose pitched up where the wings could fly."

(overleaf) Two for the show—the B-24 Diamond 'Lil with the tailguns of the B-29 Fifi in the foreground. The two CAF airplanes travel together on tour each year giving millions a chance to see them in flight.

(left) Diamond 'Lil *is an LB-30, the 18th production model off the Consolidated Aircraft assembly line.*

Full view of the B-24 Diamond 'Lil *cockpit.*

Diamond 'Lil's *Pratt & Whitney 1830 engines blow smoke as they fire for flight.*

The Douglas A-20 Havoc.

If it was tough you were after, the B-26 had it to spare. It initially featured two 1,850-horsepower Wasp engines (later increased to 2,000 horsepower) with four-bladed Curtiss propellers, a double bomb bay that could hold 4,800 pounds, self-sealing fuel tanks, and 555 pounds of armor.

For shorter-range missions and lower-altitude bombing, the two-engine B-26 and its sister ship, the Mitchell B-25, were superior to the four-engine heavies in speed, and that was of definite importance when a German Me 109 was on your tail.

Just ask any B-26 tailgunner.

A bomb tonnage of 169,000 pounds dropped during almost 130,000 B-26 sorties (a sortie is one flight flown by one airplane) earned the Martin Marauder the distinction of having the lowest combat-loss rate of any bomber involved in the war—only one percent.

Then, just a few years after it had entered the war, it was all over.

The last wartime mission was flown.

The last Nazi ammunition plants had felt the B-26s pounding them into rubble.

The last Japanese-held island had been strafed.

The last B-26 tailgunner stowed his "fifty."

And the last of the old Marauders came home to die.

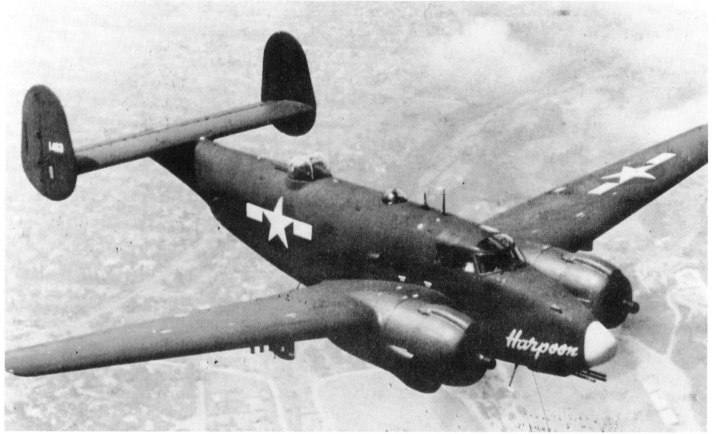

The Lockheed PV-2 anti-submarine patrol bomber.

It would be a slower death for these planes than for some others. Just as some four-engine craft found limited futures in airline service and other civilian use, a few practical applications of the B-26s were found in corporate and commercial use. (Also, in 1948, the B-26 designation passed to the Douglas Invader.)

However, higher operating costs and the difficult-to-fly image, perhaps unfairly earned in the plane's early days, assured its eventual civilian demise.

Like the young women from Avenger Field, it never seemed to get the credit it deserved.

> *We can be certain the techniques and materiel of armed conflict with which this war begins will in most cases be outmoded when it closes.*
>
> General Hap Arnold, 1940

No one argued then, nor would any argue now, the accuracy of Arnold's prediction. In truth, many of the airplanes of World War II were built with a life expectancy of as little as seven hours—one full mission. To suggest

The Douglas B-26.

(overleaf) The Martin B-26 Carolyn, once deemed "the airplane nobody loves," is now the only flying Martin B-26 in the world.

"If you were a jug pilot you felt you were invincible."
—P-47 fighter pilot Jack Terzian

that they could fly fifty or more years would have been thought insane.

In 1946, in Arnold's final paper presented on behalf of aviation, he continued to predict with uncanny accuracy the future of air power:

"The establishment of air superiority must cover every modern means of waging air war, and the techniques of employing such means must be continuously developed and kept up to date.

"An air force is always verging on obsolescence. National safety would be endangered by an air force whose doctrines and techniques are tied solely to the equipment and processes of the moment.

"The problems that may have to be faced in 1975 or 1985 will require imagination, boldness, and the utilization of available skills, manpower, and resources.

"Present equipment is but a step in progress and any air force that does not keep its doctrines ahead of its equipment, and its vision far into the future, can only delude the nation into a false sense of security.

"Prompt and speedy disposal of surpluses is a keystone to our postwar progress. The surplus of airplanes will be disposed of in a manner that will not disorganize the aircraft industry."

Now, 5,157 B-26s after Arnold wrote these words, only one authentic B-26 Martin Marauder is still flying.

It was purchased for $11,000. A paltry sum when compared with the $50,000 for the B-17 and $24,000 for the B-24 Liberator the Confederate Air Force had acquired the same year.

Republic P-47 Thunderbolts and P-51 Mustangs disassembled and ready for overseas assignments. Women Air Service Pilots tested and ferried these and other WWII aircraft from factories to ports for shipment to the front lines.

The U.S. Army gave Orville and Wilbur Wright $25,000 in 1909 to build a heavier-than-air craft that would fly 40 miles per hour. When the Wright plane averaged 42 miles per hour, the Army gave the Wright brothers a $5,000 bonus.

Three months after Pearl Harbor, $10,000 would buy a primary trainer plane. Cartoonists pictured smiling taxpayers writing their income tax return checks for 1942 with captions such as "Maybe this will pay for the gadget that releases the bomb on a plane that might be flying over Hitler!"

Tax office after tax office reported that citizens were literally rushing to file returns and people were refusing to take perfectly legitimate deductions and refunds. The reason?

National defense. Taxpayers were informed that:

A four-engine bomber cost $220,000.
A Browning machine gun cost $450.
A rear admiral's pay for one year was $8,000.
An Army lieutenant's pay for one year was $2,400.
An Army private's pay for one month was $21.

It's hot, it's noisy, and it smells. You just love every minute of it.

B-26 Restoration Project Leader Jerry Harville

The B-24 was said to have been built around a bomb bay, while the B-17 was built around a wing. The CAF Liberator was originally an LB-30 and the eighteenth airplane off the production line. It had been owned by

The Grumann F7F Tigercat never saw wartime service. The single-pilot fighter with its distinctive snout radar nose was also designed as an interceptor with a high rate of climb.

Pemex Oil Company of Mexico and was in good condition when flown to its new home as part of the CAF heavy bomber fleet.

The B-26 was also flyable when it left Denver, Colorado, where it had seen service with a private company, but that was about all that could be said of it as an authentic Marauder. In the January-February 1977 issue of the CAF *Dispatch* magazine, an article appeared with this headline:

"MARTIN B-26 MARAUDER... The Airplane Nobody Loves."

That headline did not sit well with some CAF members any more than the airplane-only-its-mother-could-love slogan did with former B-26 tailgunners, WASPs (Women Air Service Pilots), and knowledgeable B-26 pilots.

However, the condition of this particular B-26 *was* deplorable.

The plane had been heavily modified, almost beyond recognition. It had suffered major damage to the right wing spar in a ground accident in 1969. For more than nine years, it had been the victim of neglect. Landing accidents during the plane's civilian corporate service left extensive damage to the underbelly skin and formers.

It had one other major problem: no restoration funds.

And of course, like Job, the B-26 had an entourage of doubters.

It will never fly again.

It will never even look the way it did.

There will never be enough money to restore it.

If it's true that doubt is of the Devil, the Devil had now joined the Confederate Air Force.

And, like the "still, small voice" Elijah the prophet had heard, the power of the B-26 restoration began with a whisper that turned into a shout. In 1977 $7,120 was expended on the B-26 project. The next year $36,199 was spent, most of it in sheet-metal work. The money kept coming... $26,874... $35,213... $58,338..... The volunteers worked on, in what was described as a "touch-and-go" footrace between income and expenditures in order to meet the restoration financial requirement.

How is money raised to finance aircraft restoration?

The Confederate Air Force receives no local, state, or federal tax funds with which to operate. Money comes from aircraft-sponsorship donations (exact amounts are set for a sponsorship of each aircraft), membership dues, donations by private individuals, businesses, and foundations, and through various fund-raising activities. The B-26 project is a good example of the mix of the methods and skills needed to get the job done:

> Barbeque suppers paid for gun blisters.
>
> Potluck dinners paid for paint.
>
> Money earned from selling scraps of metal from damaged sections of the aircraft helped pay for the re-covering of control surfaces.
>
> Auctions, garage sales, and even blood donations brought in money from B-26 believers worldwide.
>
> Someone suggested that the only thing the group hadn't tried was opening a house of ill repute, and according to restoration project leader Jerry Harville, "there were desperate times when even *that* was considered."
>
> One man donated the gold from his teeth fillings.
>
> One woman donated her mother's wedding ring.
>
> A group of WASPs donated money in memory of two women pilots who had been killed while ferrying aircraft. "They didn't get the glory the men got, but they were just as proud," said one.

When weeks and months passed with little or no visible restoration on the B-26, the doubters would return. They quickly learned that aircraft

The Boeing B-9 Bomber was the first of the all-metal, low-wing types, and was faster than the fighters of its day.

Navy tails and folded wings ready to perform without fear of flak from the enemy.

restoration progress isn't always apparent to the casual observer.

The entire B-26 hydraulic system was completely rebuilt and certified. The rubber fuel bladders were removed, repaired, recertified, and reinstalled.

Nose gear doors had to be remanufactured, main gear doors reskinned, rounded wing tips built from scratch, navigator's station, seat, and table built and installed, bomb bay bulkhead and door returned to original configuration.

Gun turrets were installed, glass nose formed, rear gunner windows and doors built, engines donated and overhauled, an original auxiliary power unit repaired and readied for installation, control cables and vacuum lines produced, Pitot tubes built . . . the job seemed endless. Each part replaced often revealed two more needing replacement or restoration—which would be done mostly by volunteers who were never even reimbursed the wages of a 1941 Army private.

An F4U Corsair brings up the rear awaiting its turn to fly again.

Doubters are an aircraft restorer's worst enemy.

Doubters give up; restorers give out.

However, there is a place for doubters in aircraft restoration. Someone must always count the cost. Someone must believe only what can be seen. Someone must know all the reasons it can't be done. Otherwise, it would be difficult to enumerate the negative situations that must be handled.

When they painted "Carolyn" on the perfectly restored nose of the world's only authentic flying B-26 Martin Marauder, fired its twin R-2800 Pratt & Whitney engines, and flew off five years and almost $500,000 later, the B-26 Confederate Air Force restorers designated a place for all those doubters who had sided with the Devil to keep the magnificent Marauder's spirit out of the sky:

The restorers told them they could all go to hell.

Sergeant J.S. Wilson
paints a design on the
prow of a bomber.

*When you are too old
to cut the mustard,
you can still lick the jar.*

Jack Flores, West Texas CAF supporter, 1990

*F*lamin' Mamie, *Mama Foo Foo*, and *Sleepy Time Gal* made it.
Dangerous Dolores, *Buzzin' Betsy*, and *Paper Doll* didn't.

Men journey to the maintenance hangar at Confederate Air Force headquarters looking for their old sweethearts. Some even bring their wives
with them hoping to introduce them to the "ladies" they spent the war with.

Only a few of the gray-haired seekers are lucky enough to step inside
the hangar and find the gal they left behind.

Hanging along the walls are the last remnants of America's greatest pinups.
Time has faded their beauty. These pieces of nose art were full fuselages
for B-24 Liberators, B-17 Flying Fortresses, and B-29 Superfortresses.

The rest of the airplanes to which they were once attached are gone.

These World War II "ladies" owe their survival to a man who simply
wanted to be a cowboy and had no idea he was preserving a collection
of national historic significance.

His name was Minot Pratt. He was the general manager for the Aircraft

Conversion Company of Walnut Ridge, Arkansas.

Not all World War II surplus planes met their demise in the smelters of Arizona. The Aircraft Conversion Company was the end of the line for many Pacific-theater surplus aircraft. At one time, the Walnut Ridge company owned more aircraft than the United States government, with enough fuel still in the tanks to pay for the entire salvage fleet.

It was Pratt's responsibility to supervise the meltdown of postwar prop-driven airplanes. Pratt was a dedicated employee. But he could not bring himself to destroy the "fuselage flirts" painted on the noses of these airplanes destined for oblivion. Pratt had plans to eventually move to Texas and operate a cattle ranch. The nose art, he decided, would make an interesting fence at the ranch. So he ordered the paintings fire-axed from the planes before the gutted hulks were melted and turned into window screens.

A maintenance man who was good at painting pinup girls in World War II could sometimes get $50 for doing both sides of the fuselage. These paintings became known as the Glory Girls of World War II. The idea may have come from the days of the great sailing ships, when images of women were sometimes carved into the boats' bowsprits to protect sailors from the sirens of the sea. Exactly where the idea of painting women on the fuselages, noses, and sometimes tails of the aircraft started is unknown, as is the name of the first artist to risk his rank for doing so. But the idea quickly caught on, and this new art form soon became commonplace.

The names given the girls ranged from the vicious to the vulgar, from the delicate to the demeaning: *Death Angel, Photo Fanny, Liddle Lambsy Divie, Strawberry Bitch.*

Attempts were made within the Army Air Corps to stop the nose-art painting, but to no avail. Aircrew morale was too important. When a B-24 taxied into position it wasn't just another airplane about to fly a mission—it was *Delectable Doris* or *Miss Hap.* The nose art became the symbol of the group's pride and dedication. No aircrew dared fail to do its best in a plane honoring a wife, sweetheart, or dreamgirl.

But not all nose art was female. Among the male identities were "The Old Man" himself, General Hap Arnold, *Knute Rockne, Play Boy, Whisker Kid,* and *Gas House Gus.* Female names, such as *Tucson Tessie, Lonesome Lady,* and *Slick Chick* did, however, predominate.

Although Hollywood pinups were used extensively as models, it was the superb airbrush paintings of Alberto Varga (best known through his monthly beauties in *Esquire* magazine) that were most frequently copied on B-24 noses.

Spirit of Waco *A-26.*

B-24s were not the only aircraft adorned with nose art. Varga's "Pistol Packin' Mama" pinup, which appeared in *Esquire* in 1944, became *Fort Worth Gal* on a B-17. *Miss Behave* graced a P-47 Thunderbolt; *Feisty Sue* rode into combat on a P-51 Mustang.

By today's standards of erotica, Varga's scantily clad (or unclad) young women might seem tame. Although his beauties were undeniably sexy, they imparted a wholesome air as well. His treatment was tasteful, and his artwork superb (and still avidly collected today). During the war in Korea, however, the nose-art drawings began to lose their wholesomeness, and the decision to forbid individual portraits painted on the airplanes brought the practice to a close.

The exact number of painted pinups is unknown. But a World War II crew chief staging aircraft out of Herrington Field, Kansas, kept a notebook of the names and the ladies drawn on the fuselages. His list reached well over a hundred in a matter of days. He noted that often the paintings were the same with different identities, or the identities were the same with different women.

Bottoms Up.

Dozens of *Fancy Nancy* fuselages hit the skies. But Nancy was blonde, brunette, or redhead, depending on the artist who drew her. Whether she was buxom at the top or broad at the bottom, the message the artist conveyed came through loud and clear: the airplane was a girl worth fighting to save and the aircrews better not forget it.

That was how Sergeant Roy Kowalik felt when he painted *Miss Mitchell* on the side of a B-25J assigned to duty on the Island of Corsica. The original *Miss Mitchell* completed 135 combat missions and earned the 380th Squadron of the 310th Bomb Group a Presidential Unit Citation.

B-25J number 493 arrived in Corsica in April 1944. Placed in the care of a young Minnesota crew chief named Ostlie, the airplane was readied for combat.

The tactics of the missions flown by the medium bombers had changed. Low-level sweeps that the B-25 G and H models with their 75-mm cannon were so well suited for were drying up as Axis shipping dwindled. Targets were changed to power stations, highways, and troop concentrations.

Preparation for combat included removal of the "cheek pack" machine

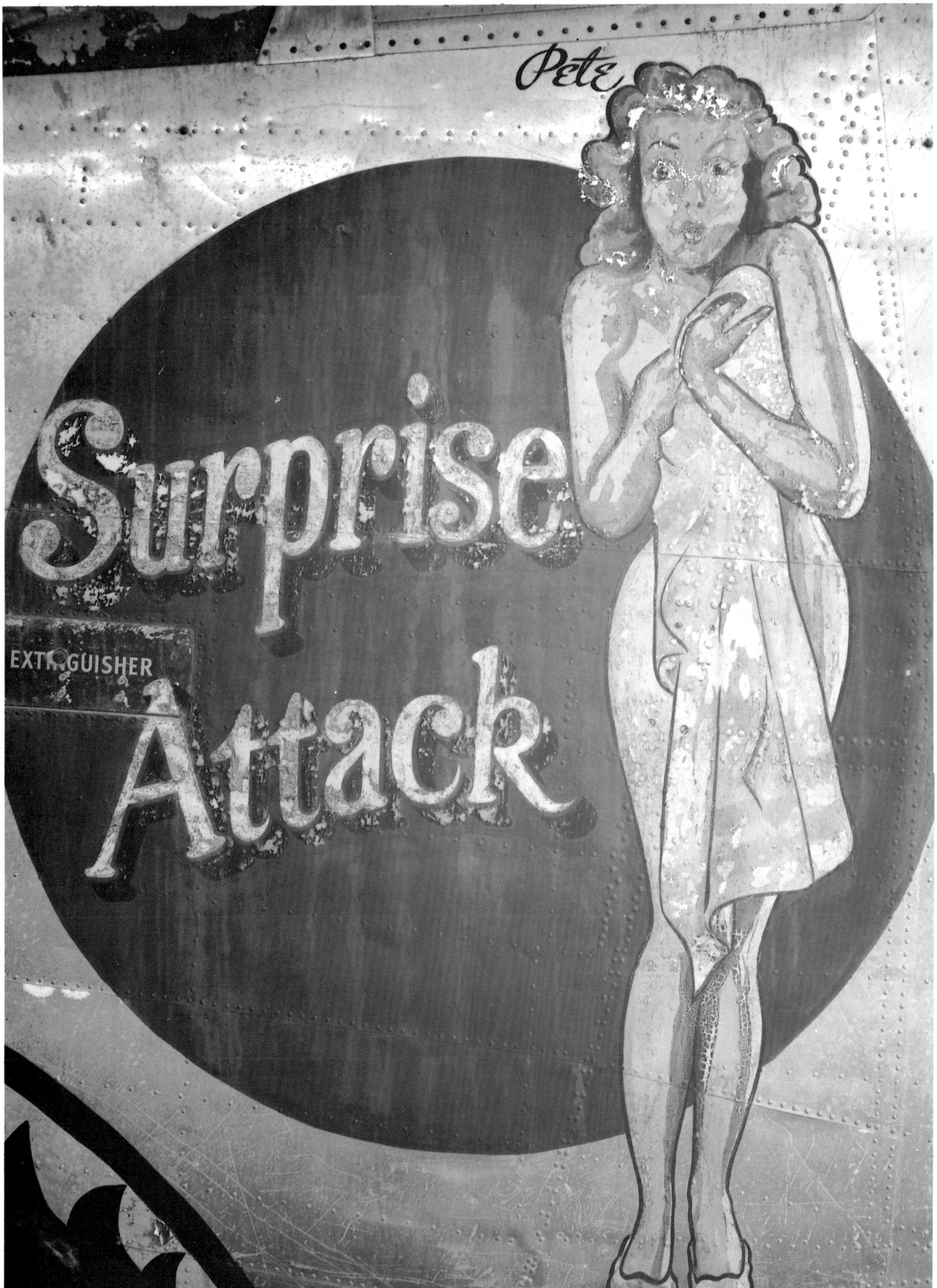
Pete
Surprise Attack
EXTINGUISHER

Sack Time.

guns, standard on the new J models. Oxygen and de-icer systems were removed because they posed a fire hazard. Two stripes were added to the vertical stabilizers. A twelve-inch yellow band on top indicated the 310th Bomb Group, while the four-inch medium-blue band beneath it indicated the 380th Squadron. Prop domes were also painted medium blue.

It was decided to give "493" a more personal identity. Someone displayed the Varga centerfold from the December 1943 issue of *Esquire* and, while everyone agreed the beautiful blonde in the red swimsuit would do just fine, the actual name was a point of contention.

Sergeant Ostlie would not, in good upstanding Minnesota fashion, let anything even resembling crudity adorn one of the first unpainted B-25s on the field. He held out for the name *Miss Mitchell* in honor of World War I aviation pioneer Billy Mitchell, who was among the first to plead for building American air superiority in the skies. After some discussion, *Miss Mitchell* she was.

Roy Kowalik, an instrument specialist on the crew of 493, had painted many noses for other aircraft and was asked to do one more. He worked

The C-47 Black Sparrow *was designed as the DC-3 before WWII. It is best known today as the "Gooney Bird" and several are still in cargo service around the world.*

A B-29 boasts A Broad With Eleven Yanks.

evenings by flashlight after his regular day's work, until *Miss Mitchell* took her position on the B-25.

Instead of being just a serial number, 493 had—with Kowalik's paintbrush—become one of the nation's Glory Girls.

After the war *Miss Mitchell* was destroyed as part of a weapons-testing program in Maryland. Like the old Hellcat in Arizona, it was still a better fate for a proud Lady than the smelters.

The B-25 chosen as a restoration project by the Southern Minnesota Wing of the Confederate Air Force never flew a combat mission overseas. But it was nonetheless an important part of the Allied victory of the skies as a stateside trainer. It managed to escape smelters and weapons testing and eventually was owned by a physician in Wisconsin, who donated the bomber to the CAF in 1980.

Not only would the Southern Minnesota Wing restore a B-25 to the configuration of the original *Miss Mitchell*; they decided to find the artist

B-17 Texas Raiders.

who painted the nose art on the original aircraft and have him draw again the exact image of the beautiful blonde whose honor was protected through 135 combat missions. And so it happened that, almost a half-century later, Roy Kowalik repeated his loving task.

To have the original artist re-create his original drawing on the same type of aircraft forty-five years later was a restoration first.

"In every restoration project there are firsts," a dedicated project officer explains. "What you're hoping to avoid is ever doing something for the *last* time. Some restoration is an ongoing, never-ending process. You have to believe there will always be others to come along behind you and do the work when it needs to be done again. You know what you do today won't last forever.

"You have to believe there will always be people who love the airplanes enough to keep them flying."

Aircraft restoration requires meticulous research just as much as it requires

A-26 Daisy Mae.

DANGER

Razor

CREW CHIEFS
Col. Jerald
Col. Doug

When Sentimental Journey *was ready to return to flying status, bandleader Harry James gave his personal permission for his wife Betty Grable's famous pin-up shot to be painted on the B-17's nose.*

meticulous craftsmanship. Whether locating a ball turret or locating the artist who drew the original *Miss Mitchell*, no restoration could be accomplished without those who dig through old logbooks, sift through archives, decipher faded handwriting, and haunt dimly lighted rooms prowling dusty boxes of memorabilia.

Aircraft restoration researchers are often stooped and seldom satisfied; they squint from reading fine print and their fingers are stained with old ink rather than grease.

Each crumbling document is a new possibility that they will uncover what everyone else has missed.

Aircraft restoration researchers dot their *i*'s and cross their *t*'s, and they are annoyed by those who do not. They are intimately acquainted with every design modification an aircraft has undergone, including the ones that never made it past the drawing boards.

While the names or initials of some of the Confederate Air Force nose-art painters are known, other information about them is scarce.

Drake, Zord, Silva, Pete . . . .

They are faceless artisans whose work brought meaning to the cruel madness of war and now brings delight to a new generation of viewers who come to the CAF hangar.

Roy Kowalik was located through a directory of crew members who flew B-25s in the Mediterranean. He agreed to paint the newly restored *Miss Mitchell* with the understanding that it would be done as authentically as possible, right down to the flashlight.

Minot Pratt moved to Brackettville, Texas, to start his cattle company with a partner named Slim Dahlstrom. The fuselage portions he had salvaged were stored in a barn at nearby Fort Clark Springs for the next twenty years. For all practical purposes their final viewers seemed destined to be cows, coyotes, and jackrabbits.

But Tully Pratt, Minot's son, had other ideas. Tully had seen several Confederate Air Force shows, and he realized his father's fence makings deserved historic preservation.

Arrangements were made. In the mid-1960s about thirty pieces of one-of-a-kind nose art were delivered from the Fort Clark barn to CAF headquarters, where they were hoisted high along the inside of the maintenance hangar walls.

They say it isn't unusual on Valentine's Day for florists to arrive at the hangar bearing bouquets of flowers with cards addressed to *Sack Time, Double Trouble,* or *Sleepytime Gal.*

The senders are old, gray-haired men who were once B-24 pilots or B-17 crew chiefs.

And the cards are always signed, "With love."

Should the fading nose art be repainted?

The authenticity of the paintings will be compromised, say those who object to even touching up the flimsy nightie of *Mission Accomplished* or the strategically placed towel held by *Surprise Attack.*

But others feel restoration of the nose art, like restoration of the aircraft, is essential to preserving it.

Amid the flak generated by these diverse viewpoints, the painted women keep silent. Where they've been and the men they've known are secrets every aircraft restoration researcher would give his spiral notebook to find out.

But they are Glory Girls.

And a Glory Girl *never* tells.

*Whoever rules
the air will win the war
and will dictate
the peace.*

1942 Vultee Aircraft advertisement

May 1983. Nelson Ezell scratched his head behind his right ear.

It was a familiar gesture to his fellow workers at Breck Airways in Breckenridge, Texas. They had seen it many times when an old airplane arrived at the West Texas facility in need of repairs or rebuilding.

But they had never seen him scratch this hard.

Piled unceremoniously on a flatbed trailer in front of the Breck hangar at Stephens County Airport were hundreds of pieces of twisted metal, dangling hoses, and debris shattered almost beyond recognition.

Ezell, William Morgan, and the other war-bird mechanics and restorers recognized the pile all too well: the trailer held all that remained of the world's last, authentic flying SB2C Helldiver.

Considered the rarest of all the Confederate Air Force fleet, the cantankerous Curtiss-built SB2C-5 had joined the Ghost Squadron in 1971. It had been purchased for $25,000 by an individual who immediately donated it to the CAF collection. Just before Airsho '82 (the CAF's annual air-power

(overleaf) This SB2C-5 bears the markings of the carrier Franklin. *Restoration costs of the only flying "Beast" in the world totalled $164,000 and more than 6,000 hours of work.* 121

Row on row of SBD engines inside the Douglas Aircraft plant at El Segundo, California.

demonstration), the Big-Tailed Beast, which was being used as a camera ship, crashed into a plowed field in South Texas.

Now, clods of dirt and grass sprouting from the metal shards gave mute testimony that the wreckage had been given up for dead.

It wasn't the first time the SB2C seemed destined for the scrap heap.

The Navy Bureau of Aeronautics began looking for a successor to the SBD Dauntless in 1938. The Scout-Bomber request included the following requirements:

> use of the Wright R-2600 Cyclone 14 engine; increased internal fuel capacity; bomb bay capable of holding a 1,000-pound bomb; and size small enough to allow two planes to fit on a 40′ × 48′ aircraft-carrier elevator with a foot to spare in all directions.

This last requirement was to plague the Helldiver from its very beginning. Increasing the width meant increasing the tail size to compensate for the plane's lack of stability. The first Helldiver prototype looked like "fifty pounds of potatoes in a ten-pound sack."

When wind-tunnel tests indicated excessive stall speeds, the wing was quickly redesigned. In December 1940 a contract was issued for 340 dive bombers—an airplane completely untested.

Low speed, marginal stability in pitch, and failure of the right wing and tail that resulted in the sole prototype crashing in a test flight a year after the planes were ordered are all factors that would have been the airplane's finish even before it started, except for one thing:

America was at war.

"Pearl Harbor converted our long-deliberated plan of action into action itself. In the sudden transformation from a nation at peace to a nation at war, our air program was like an animal unleashed from its cage after long confinement, but with neither his teeth nor claws sharp enough or strong enough to be immediately effective," General Arnold wrote after the war.

Instead of giving up on the Helldiver, the Navy elected to sharpen its teeth and claws.

Before the first production SB2C-1 finally rolled off the Columbus, Ohio assembly line, 4,000 Helldivers had been ordered. The SB2C-1 had met the original critical requirements, but the trade-off in reduced performance was phenomenal. Empty weight rose from 7,122 to 10,144 pounds, top speed dropped from 320 to 280 knots, and landing speed rose from 69 to 79 knots.

Modification replaced modification. While many of the 800 mods were not outwardly visible, the huge tail of the "Beast" kept growing.

It was a production nightmare. Nonetheless, the Navy was determined to get the Helldiver into service as quickly as possible. The carrier *Essex* took on the first squadrons, but too many problems were found and operations were never begun.

A congressional investigation in 1943 revealed that not a single SB2C was usable as a combat airplane. Its critics argued that the plane should be killed.

The Navy refused to budge. Instead, it ordered more modifications.

The SB2Cs were bestowed upon the reluctant carrier *Yorktown*. Predictable disasters followed. Hook-bounce and landing-gear failures were so common that the carrier's forward barriers could not be repaired quickly enough before frustrated dive bomber pilots rammed them again while trying to land their slow, heavy "Beasts."

People say the *Yorktown* captain suggested that Helldivers be redesignated as anchors and permanently sunk. But the Navy persisted.

The SB2C-3 design boasted a 1,900-horsepower R-2600-20 Cyclone

Two SB2Cs and a Corsair are destined for final destruction in the smelters.

with a four-bladed propeller. In June 1944, 2,045 of the SB2C-4 production model had been built, with wing fittings for eight five-inch rockets or 1,000 pounds of additional bombs, perforated flaps, and radar.

By the time the SB2C-5 variant was under production, the Helldiver's popularity tide had turned. Its longer range and deadly accuracy were distinct advantages in the Pacific's enormous watery battlefields.

The "Bombing Banshees" were the first Marines to take the Helldiver into combat against the Japanese at Mindanao in June 1945. They quickly proved that the plane's capabilities had finally achieved what the Navy had been looking for when it began producing it at the start of the war.

"In the future we will be able to avoid the mistake of producing airplanes that have not yet been tested," said Artemas Gates, Assistant Secretary of the Navy for Air, in his report of June 30, 1945.

"When we needed the SB2C neither we nor it was ready. Thanks to the spirit of our people and our airplanes, we won a war with our mistakes as well as with our victories."

Production of the SB2C-5s began in February 1945, but only a few reached active duty before the war's end. There were 970 built before the Navy cancelled production.

"The Navy finally admitted they didn't like the Helldiver," a carrier pilot

Stack-up, right-echelon formation of T-6 gunnery trainers. Note the rear cockpit machine-gun position.

SB2C, May 23, 1945.

remarked. "But they also knew it was a damn good thing *we* had it instead of the Japanese."

The airplane is fundamentally composed of three major components: the airframe, the engine and the propeller. All else on the airplane comes under the heading of accessories or equipment.

The load-carrying structure of an airplane—the airframe— includes wings, fuselage, and control surfaces and the metallic or fabric skin that covers them.

Aluminum alloy, alclad and stainless steel are the basic materials most commonly used in airframes.

Alclad, which is an aluminum-alloy sheet with pure aluminum coating, is used for skin covering.

Aluminum alloy is used for ribs, structural parts of wings and fuselages, cowlings and longerons.

Stainless steel is used for parts, such as engine mounts and firewalls, which must withstand high temperatures. Some wing panels are being built of stainless steel. Even within the basic components of the airframe there are many intricate parts and construction details.

For example, in the metal wing tip of a P-38, there are 14 pieces of tubing, ribs and sheet skin, and 277 bolts and nuts plus hundreds of rivets.

Official Army Air Force Guide, 1944

Rivets. Rivets. And more rivets.

Don't ask William Morgan how many rivets are in an SB2C-5 unless you really want to know. Morgan is an airframe and power-plant mechanic for Ezell Aviation (formerly Breck Airways).

He's one of those detail people not content to say what he can't back up with the paperwork.

The firewall of an SB2C-5.

Another view.

Dive brakes on the SB2C were used to slow the airplane during dives and to provide a more stable bombing platform. The SBD dive bomber, which the SB2C was designed to replace, also used the same type of dive brakes.

This Wright R-2600 engine for the restored SB2C was found unused in its original crate in the back of a hangar in Ozona, Texas.

The SB2C's tail hook required several modifications before it satisfied carrier commanders who did not like the airplane and objected to having it on their ships.

The cockpit of the SB2C after completely being refurbished.

The only flying SB2C in the world was restored from the scrap pile and returned to service through the efforts of the CAF West Texas Wing.

When the trailer with the remains of the Confederate Air Force Helldiver arrived at Stephens County Airport in 1983, Morgan knew the members of the West Texas wing under the leadership of Bob Richeson and the Cactus Squadron had taken on a project of major proportions.

The airframe rebuild would entail complete fabrication of six feet of the fuselage section. At least most of the other pieces were there, Morgan noted. Three vital elements would still have to be found: an R-2600-20 engine, approximately $200,000, and plenty of time.

It wasn't the money or the time that concerned Morgan most.

It was the engine.

For eight months CAF members followed every lead and traveled every trail in search of an R-2600-20 Wright Cyclone. Rumors surfaced of engines in warehouses in Wellington, in cartons in Khartoum, and in salvage yards in South America. Each proved untrue.

Under the skillful hands and watchful eyes of Nelson Ezell, the SB2C was slowly transformed from a junk pile to a magnificent Beast. Volunteers

This SB2C-5 "Big Tailed Beast" flies again after complete restoration in Breckenridge, Texas.

labored into the dark morning hours when days were too hot to endure the hangar corner where the Beast on its jig awaited the time when it would again unfold its wings and fly.

They found the engine perfectly preserved and ready to install, still in its crate in the back of a hangar in the town of Ozona, less than two hundred miles southwest of Nelson Ezell's hangar.

They found the money the same way they found money for all the CAF restoration projects: in the pockets and purses of men and women who donated a dollar or five dollars and sometimes ten to have a part in reminding all who saw the SB2C fly that American air power had kept freedom alive in the past, and must be kept strong and equipped to do so again.

An ex-prisoner of war whose last ride in a Beast had ended in a Japanese POW camp came to Breckenridge to show his wife and grandchildren the plane with which he had met the enemy.

"I'd go through it all over again—including being a prisoner of war—just

A Grumman TBF/TBM was the largest carrier-based aircraft in WWII. It weighed up to 19,500 pounds on takeoff. The TBF was built by Grumman, the TBM by General Motors.

to fly one more good mission in that son-of-a-bitch," he said. He left Breckenridge with a thousand memories, and without his last five-dollar bill. Instead of the usual thirty or forty thousand dollars, this project ultimately cost $164,000, encompassed 6,600 paid man-hours, and required many hundreds more from volunteers.

A Gold Team sponsorship program was initiated to generate contributions of $200 toward the SB2C restoration. Anyone donating $200 was entitled to wear the Gold Team SB2C Helldiver patch. More than one hundred individuals participated, as did several entire squadrons and wings. Challenge grants from major philanthropic foundations, memorabilia sales, and untold amounts in labor and material personally donated by Ezell and his employees resulted in the SB2C flying debt-free by the close of 1989.

"By the early part of 1945 we had complete domination of the air in all naval theaters of operation in the Pacific," reported Assistant Secretary Gates after the war.

"From our own West Coast and that of South America to the East Indies, to China, and up to the very door of Japan. At this very moment Navy search and patrol planes are operating over the South China Sea,

Yellow Sea, and the Sea of Japan, as well as the southern approaches to the home islands and over the Kuriles to the north. The battle for the control of the air over Japan itself is underway.

"More than 17,000 enemy planes have been destroyed since Pearl Harbor by Navy and Marine planes against Fleet combat losses of approximately 2,700—a combat ratio of better than 6 to 1."

All totaled, in 283,755 naval sorties, 4,231 planes were lost.

On August 14, 1945, when the Japanese surrendered, the Columbus Curtiss-Wright Aircraft plant was in its twentieth consecutive month of on-schedule production of Helldivers. Special machining fixtures were designed and developed at the Columbus plant that sped by seventy percent production of engine mounts for the SB2C.

The plant got a star for its "E" Award flag, a renewal of the excellence-in-production award.

Secretary of the Navy James Forrestal in his 1945 report stated:

> "Carrier-based aircraft made 2,673 sorties in 1941. In 1945 they made 70,166. The Empire of the Rising Sun did not believe a force caught as unprepared as ours could accomplish such a feat. Their gamble cost us dearly, but nothing compared with what it cost them.
>
> "The strength of the Naval Air Force grew from 1,741 service planes to more than 39,700. While the number of naval planes lost in the Okinawa campaign would have required eight months to produce in 1941, those losses amounted to only twelve days output at the production rate of June, 1945."

On November 30, 1945, the Navy had 32,410 airplanes on hand. Of these, 3,441 were Scout Bombers.

On November 30, 1985, only one was left.

But it simply would not die.

An "E" Award flag presented to Nelson Ezell and Ezell Aviation by the West Texas Wing of the Confederate Air Force is almost hidden among the snapshots of airplanes lining the wall of the Breckenridge hangar.

William Morgan slowly closes the file-cabinet drawer containing the completed reconstruction records of the world's last flying SB2C Helldiver.

"Approximately fifteen thousand and twenty-two," he says. Fifteen thousand and twenty-two rivets in one SB2C Helldiver.

One Big-Tailed Beast.

*A vintage A-26 airplane on a test run
before heading for an air museum
to be permanently displayed
crashed less than two minutes after takeoff,
but the two pilots walked away.*

*Pilot Paul Weston was testing
the landing gear of the attack·plane
before flying it later to the
U.S. Air Force Air Museum
in Fargo, North Dakota.*

The Associated Press Wire Service, 1985

Few who read the brief news account of that A-26 Invader crash ever knew the true findings of the National Transportation Safety Board's routine investigation of the crash.

The NTSB brought in their best experts to try to figure out such things as why the engine "just went out" a minute after takeoff, and why the landing gear wouldn't retract to give Weston time to make it back to the airport only a mile away.

Weston said that "she started to go over on her back," and the experts wanted to know why. They aerodynamically reconstructed every flight characteristic of her 1941 design.

The Douglas Invader had a proud history. It had been one of very few aircraft entirely conceived, designed, developed, produced in quantity, and used in large numbers all during World War II.

Its glory didn't end there. Some 450 were used in Korea, and in Vietnam they were the most favored platforms for night attack on the Ho Chi Minh Trail.

The A-26 on takeoff roll.

Pulling the three-blade props through on the massive R-2800 engines of the A-26 is a three-man job.

An A-26 with a nose full of guns.

The Douglas A-26 with its solid nose saw service late in WWII and survived to fly in Korea and Vietnam.

Unlike so many of her sisters, the Invader did not die out when World War II no longer needed her.

But thirty years in combat is a long time. It can do strange things to men—and machines.

According to the Associated Press, "Harry Wilson, a farmer who owns the land where the crash occurred, said he heard the plane making a lot of noise, looked up, and saw it flying just above treetop level."

Naturally. The A-26 was never noted for being quiet. With its bodacious double-slotted flaps and remote-control turrets and powered by two 2,000-horsepower engines, it had always been an attention getter.

Yessir, she was determined to go out with a bang, kindly clipping a tree with one wing to soften the blow and allowing the two somewhat helpless occupants to calmly walk away.

Of course, the NTSB puzzled over the fact that the plane broke up on impact and, although fully fueled, didn't burn. And they could not come up with any plausible explanation why Weston's attempt to increase power wouldn't keep her in the air.

The NTSB eventually arrived at a very accurate technical explanation for the A-26 crash that clear day. But those who know old airplanes have their own opinion.

It was simply the A-26's last chance to die with dignity.

*The actual end of the war in Europe
brought little elation to the fighting men.
All romance and adventure had gone from war,
even in the air. It was big business,
a great and grinding effort
day in and day out for millions.*

*Europe was only a part of the great war,
and the men in Europe turned to the Far East with little to say.
They did not want to go, but there was a job to be done.
The final ransom would have to be paid to settle
the debt that began at Pearl Harbor.*

*They would do it with the help of God,
the American people, the Allied support
and the B-29 Superfortresses.*

General Hap Arnold, 1945

That day in 1961 at the Aerospace Vehicles Distribution office of the USAF Logistics Command headquarters at Wright-Patterson Air Force Base, the clerk sat opening the mail. He had not even been born when the Twentieth Air Force was created solely for using the Superfortress bombers to get to the very heart of the Japanese industrial centers. He laughed and shook his head.

"These people want to know if any B-29s are still available at our disposal facilities. They don't want it for display—they want to fly it!"

It wasn't so unusual anymore for the Vehicle Distribution office to receive requests from groups and individuals looking for aircraft or aircraft parts for restoration projects. Interest in war-bird flying had been growing steadily.

From California to Florida, individuals and organizations pooled efforts and resources to rebuild and maintain what was left of four years of aviation history.

America's airplanes were not the only ones of interest. Wright-Patterson regularly received requests for help in locating aircraft built by Axis as well as Allied nations. Spitfires, Messerschmitts, Junkers—the search was on.

The clerk had heard of the Confederate Air Force and their efforts to restore at least one of each major World War II aircraft to authentic flying configuration. These aviators were obviously serious about expanding their flying collection if they intended to include not only trainers and fighters but bombers as well.

A response was dutifully dispatched:

The Air Force had no B-29s left in its inventory.

At the end of the war some 2,865 B-29s were still in service. The bomber that stunned the Land of the Rising Sun for months before dropping the atomic bomb had outperformed even the best estimates of its designers.

In 1938 a study for a new bomber with pressurized cabin and tricycle landing gear had begun. This evolved into model 345, which carried a crew of ten to fourteen with four 2,200-horsepower Wright R-3350-23 Duplex 18-cylinder radials, each with two exhaust-driven turbochargers.

It had a wingspan of 141 feet, 3 inches, a length of 99 feet, and weighed in at 74,500 pounds empty, 135,000 pounds loaded.

By all previous comparisons, the B-29 was astounding.

"I remember seeing the tail sticking up over the palm trees at Harlingen while I was in basic training," said a young crash-crew airman. "I could not imagine how anything that big could fly."

The B-29 required not only the imagination of Boeing Aircraft engineers but the combined involvement of Bell, North American, Fisher (General Motors), and—later on—Martin. Almost four thousand were delivered, and in 1944 they began making Japan bleed internally for the first time.

By July of 1945, bomb loads carried by the Superfortress had increased from 2.6 to 7.4 tons. The Twenty-First Bomber Command flew 90 million miles to and from the Japanese mainland, with an accident loss rate of slightly more than one plane for every million miles flown. The percentage of airborne craft lost on bombing missions dropped from a high of 5.7 percent in January to 0.4 percent in July.

The B-29 airmen became steadily more independent of weather or

(overleaf) B-29 Fifi *in a low pass over Dyess Air Force Base, Abilene, Texas.*

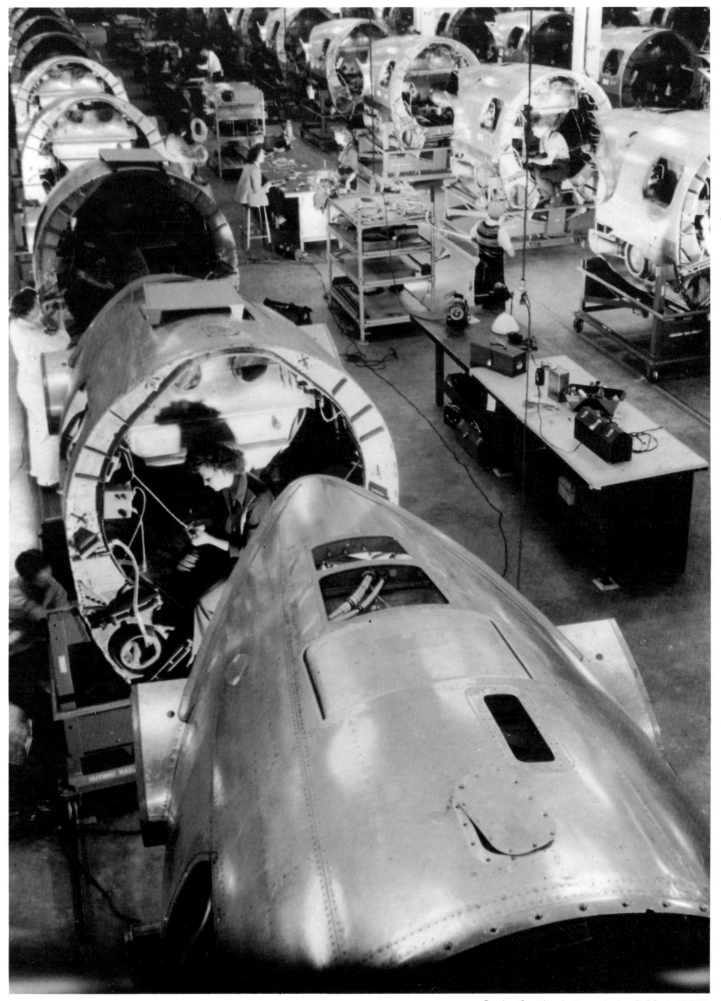

Boeing Seattle plant producing B-29s in WWII.

The B-29 Fifi is ready for another morning's flight.

(overleaf)
*The only flying B-29
in the world covers
West Texas on tour
for the CAF.*

B-29 engines and props.

natural vision, and more a day-or-night air force. In July 1945, the record month of B-29 effort, more than 75 percent of all bomb releases were radar-guided.

In March, Major General Curtis LeMay, then commanding the Twenty-First Bomber Command, made one of the most important decisions of the war—to attack Tokyo with incendiaries at low level at night with full force.

In no previous operation, night or day, had B-29s bombed from altitudes of less than 24,000 feet; but on the night of March 9, 279 B-29s attacked Tokyo at a mean bombing altitude of 7,050 feet.

The Japanese defenses were confused. Amazingly, only fourteen B-29s were lost to all causes. Some 15.8 square miles of the heart of Tokyo was burned out in what was, before the atomic bomb, the most destructive air attack in history. And still the Japanese would not surrender.

A master plan had been completed, one that called for invasions of Japan at three points simultaneously. Japan's home forces numbered well over two million troops. They still had between five thousand and ten thousand planes. It was clear that these would be used as kamikaze weapons and make an invasion very costly in human lives. Only one alternative existed.

B-29s abandoned in the desert.

At 8:15 A.M. Japanese time, on August 6, 1945, one bomb was dropped from the bomb bay of a single B-29 over Hiroshima. Three days later, another was dropped over Nagasaki. Together, they brought World War II to a sudden end. Unbelievable death and destruction resulted. It would ultimately save an estimated one and one-half million human lives that would have been lost had invading the Japanese homeland been necessary.

This one event showed all mankind a weapon of such destructive force as to make all future wars unthinkable.

Early in 1966 the Confederate Air Force received a letter from a pilot who had seen aircraft resembling B-29s parked in a remote area of Maryland.

There had been other leads, all deadends. But what would it hurt to follow up on just one more?

153

This one proved to be true. There *were* B-29s, at least in some form or fashion, located at the Aberdeen proving grounds. They belonged to the Department of the Army and were being used as targets for weapons tests. This information was relayed back to the Air Force Logistics Command headquarters, which arranged for CAF personnel to inspect the planes. AFLC determined that the aircraft was surplus to Army needs and could be made available to the CAF.

The CAF members who went to Aberdeen to inspect the airplanes expected the worst. They were not disappointed.

Recovery would be difficult, but it appeared to be the only possibility. With some hesitation, plans were begun.

"It was hard to get enthusiastic about what we knew would be more work than any of us could hope to do in a lifetime. Not to mention the money that we sure as hell didn't have," Lloyd Nolen commented dryly.

Almost a year after the Aberdeen trip, CAF headquarters received another pilot report of craft resembling B-29s in the California desert. Project Officer Lefty Gardner dispatched California CAF member Roger Baker to proceed to China Lake, establish contact with the Navy, and arrange to inspect the aircraft.

Exactly what went through Baker's mind when he saw the California cache is unknown. But what ensued is the most inspiring story of restoration in aviation history.

Thirty-five B-29s had been left for dead in the Mojave Desert. What thieves and vandals had not stripped, the wind and sand had ground away. What thieves, vandals, wind, and sand had not destroyed, the Navy gunners had.

But the dry desert climate had also helped preserve the airplanes in better condition than those at Aberdeen. It was also revealed that the airplanes were still U.S. Air Force property and had been supplied to the Navy for use as targets. These planes could not be disposed of without prior approval of the Air Force Logistics Command.

After reams of paperwork and weeks of negotiations, the AFLC agreed that the CAF could have its choice of any of the China Lake B-29s.

CAF member Victor N. Agather, former B-29 pilot, was asked to put the project into motion by raising the necessary funds to begin restoration. Agather had played a major role in the acquisition of the CAF's B-24 Liberator.

Agather had more than a passing interest in the Superfortress. In 1941, while stationed at Wright Field, he had been selected to serve on the

These B-29 bombers dropping their loads over Korea once flew over Japan.

development staff of the B-29. He had worked with Boeing engineers and Air Corps flight test units, and in 1944 he'd flown to the Marianas Islands in the southwest Pacific with the Twentieth Air Force.

No one wanted to see the B-29 rise from its sandy grave more than Vic Agather.

It took two years to overcome finicky bureaucratic problems before a final selection was made of the craft best suited to restoration.

To the Air Force the big plane was now known simply as SN44-62070. Built by Boeing, buried by progress.

On March 31, 1971, the once-abandoned B-29 was moved from the China Lake scrap yard to a more suitable work area at the nearby air base. A private contractor was hired to do certain portions of the restoration while a group of CAF members moved west to do the rest.

The criteria for selecting number 44-62070 was basic: There had been no major structural damage and little corrosion, and some of the glass was still intact. The most important consideration was the engines.

"We didn't have a single record of any kind on the engines," said a member of the maintenance crew. "It was blind luck at best. We'd talk and look and talk and look and tell each other we were all crazy as hell to think of flying an airplane that had been sitting unprotected for seventeen years with engines we didn't know one damn thing about. Then we'd go back to work."

Over a period of nine weeks, all systems were restored; all fuel, oil, and hydraulic hoses were removed, recovered, and reinstalled. After every instrument had been put in place, engines were run and landing gear retraction tests were completed under the supervision of CAF personnel Duane Egli and J.A. McCafferty.

A short wait followed while engine accessories were overhauled and new window bubbles manufactured. CAF members volunteered days, weekends, and weeks at China Lake removing B-29 spare parts from other aircraft left in the desert.

"It always made me feel sad in a way when I removed parts from one of the old airplanes left out there because I knew that meant it would for sure never get to fly again," said one volunteer.

Early in the project a flight crew had been selected and its members had been preparing for the "test" flight—a flight that would be the only one allowed. Because of Navy regulations and the top-secret nature of the project at China Lake, the CAF crew was informed that once the plane left the runway, it could not return.

Randy Sohn of Minneapolis, along with Lefty Gardner, Roger Baker, Jim McCafferty, Darell Skurich, and contractor Jim Kern arrived at China Lake late in July. They spent several days making final preflight inspections and engine and systems checks.

At 7:48 A.M. on Tuesday, August 3, 1971, B-29 Superfortress 44-62070, loaded with enough fuel to fly nonstop to Harlingen, Texas, rumbled down the runway.

"It was a complete act of faith and confidence on our part in the superb workmanship of everyone who had had a part in getting the airplane airworthy. Our job was easy—we were just the flight crew who got to take her home," said Sohn.

Six hours and thirty-eight minutes later, with all systems functioning perfectly, the B-29 smoothly touched down at CAF headquarters.

Another chapter in the saga of the Superfortress had begun in March when the CAF officially received title to the aircraft. The title specified that the aircraft was cleared for one flight only, from China Lake to Harlingen. Any other flights were strictly prohibited.

Vic Agather headed to Washington, D.C.

Not just once or twice, but on numerous occasions, he worked to convince the Air Force that the CAF was qualified to maintain and operate the B-29, and that the U.S. Air Force itself would be the principal recipient of the benefits of the magnificent historic airplane's preservation and flight.

On November 27, 1973, the CAF received a letter from Lieutenant General Francis G. Gideon outlining the conditions that the CAF had to meet to obtain permission to fly the aircraft. One condition was that it be fully certified by the civilian Federal Aviation Administration.

Dennis Williams of Brownsville was commissioned to restore and certificate the only flying B-29 in the world. He began work on March 4, 1974, and six months later the airplane was signed off by the FAA.

With this and all other conditions established by the Air Force met, on October 10, 1974, the CAF received official permission from the Air Force to return the B-29 to service.

With a fully operational, authentic B-29 bomber, the Confederate Air Force had accomplished what no other restoration group or individual had.

Boasting a fresh paint job that cost $7001.95 and the shiniest sixteen-foot props ever turned by eighteen-cylinder Wright Cyclone engines, the plane that had been christened *FiFi* in honor of Vic Agather's wife would have a new mission: to remind the world that *no* nation can ever again afford the cost of a world war.

Our planes are making themselves understood in the tropics,
Arctic and desert; over sea, mountain and glacier.

In China, at this moment, some of us
may just be landing medium bombers
after raiding Japanese warehouses in Indochina.
Every ounce of gasoline our planes used,
like the gas for the heavy bombers just now taking off
for a dawn mission to bomb Formosa,
was carried over the Himalayas by air.
In India our transports are coming in after a day of shuttling these supplies.

Several thousand miles to the southeast
on a Pacific island once headquarters for the enemy,
others of us are being briefed to sweep over an enemy harbor
and attack his shipping.

On a tiny island in the Arabian Sea we sit out a sandstorm.
On the hot Tunisian desert we are still busy looking
for salvageable items from the year-old wrecks of enemy planes.

On the west coast of the U.S.,
while another shift is coming off work in the great airplane factories,
thousands of us are taking off in training flights
in small aircraft that outperform the
combat planes our pilots flew in the last war.

In a New York City procurement office
a request is dictated for four million rivets.
In the Aleutians the 'I Bombed Japan' club is initiating some new members.

160

We are over Kansas on our first solo;
high over central Germany with enemy fighters attacking;
low over a Japanese airfield strafing planes on the runway;
far out over the Pacific
with an enemy warship clearly fixed in the cross-hairs of our bombsight.
Let there be no mistake by our enemies…

We are a worldwide air force!

General Hap Arnold, 1944

They didn't stop with American airplanes.

By 1972 the Confederate Air Force was able to display not only a complete set of American bombers along with their fighters, but also the world's most extensive collection of other WWII aircraft of all types. The momentum of their effort brought into the CAF's operational fleet a substantial collection of fighters, bombers, transports, and trainers used between 1939 and 1945 by the Royal Air Force of Britain, the German *Luftwaffe*, and the Imperial Japanese Navy.

As early as 1974 several of these non-American planes were operational.

Now 136 aircraft, all flyable or in restoration, represent sixty-one different aircraft types flown during the war by the U.S., its allies, and its enemies.

The CAF's stated objectives were revised to reflect the additional aim of "acquiring, restoring, and preserving in flying condition a complete collection of combat aircraft that were flown by all military services of the United States, and selected aircraft of other nations, in World War II.

161

The FW 44 Stieglitz German trainer.

"The desire of the membership is to permit the collection to continue to grow, but at a slower pace. We are on the trail of other World War II types. We hear talk of a Heinkel He 111 and the trimotor Junkers Ju 52. These aircraft have been located and are in reasonably good condition.

"All that is needed to put them on the ramp is money. Anyone interested in the former who can provide some of the latter can get in on a recovery mission."

Such statements were the fuel for restoration fire.

Old "Auntie Ju" was on her way.

Resurrected by the CAF from the junkyard in Spain, the Junkers Ju 52 (also known as Iron Annie or Auntie Ju), with the Stuka and the Bf 109, had been the universal symbol of the Nazi war machine. With its three engines and a rectangular body of corrugated aluminum, crews claimed it took "two men and a large boy" just to get the clumsy Junkers started.

The Junkers 1932 design characteristics were far ahead of the times. The horizontal stabilizer trimmed automatically when the flaps were raised and lowered, contributing to the aircraft's ability to take off within a thousand

The German Heinkel He 11 was ostensibly developed as a high-speed civilian transport, but the only "fares" it collected were from its enemies.

162

(right) The Junkers Ju 52 "Iron Annie", also known as "Auntie Ju", was built in Spain. Made of corrugated aluminum, the airplane reportedly took "two men and a large boy" to start it.

The German Junkers Ju 52 needed only 1,000 feet to take off and 800 feet to land.

The swastika was boldly emblazoned on German aircraft and was particularly prominent on the vertical fin.

164

The "Spit" with its Rondel insignia.

The Spitfire of the RAF was one of the airplanes credited with saving Great Britain from the Germans.

"On top" in the British Spitfire.

feet and land within eight hundred. Authentic restoration of Auntie Ju included an instrument panel printed in Spanish with metric gauges. Altitude was measured in meters, airspeed in kilometers per hour, pressures in kilograms per square centimeter, and fuel in liters.

The Ju 52 transport, the Heinkel He 111 bomber, the Focke-Wulf 44 trainer, and the Bf 109 Messerschmitt fighter were part of Germany's wings of revenge.

The Messerschmitt prototype first flew in 1935. Ironically, it used a Rolls-Royce engine. More than thirty thousand were built, the largest number of any one combat plane in history.

The Bf 109 was a small fighter. The P-51 Mustang weighed almost twice as much. Yet for all its abilities, it had a liability no amount of pilot skill or speed could overcome—extremely limited range.

Two Bf 109s brought from Spain are now part of the Confederate Air Force, as is an Me 108.

Only eighteen years after the end of World War I, "the war to end all wars," Germany began rearming in violation of the Treaty of Versailles.

The P-40 Warhawk was the airplane made famous by Claire Chennault in the American Volunteer Group "Flying Tigers" in China.

Amid the carnage of the Spanish Civil War, Adolph Hitler's reborn German *Luftwaffe* tested its weapons in preparation for his planned conquest of Europe—and then the world.

The re-emergence of the *Luftwaffe* was accomplished in relative secrecy. To counter the regulatory controls of the Treaty of Versailles, the German aircraft industry developed bomber aircraft under the guise of civilian transports.

The Heinkel He 111 was developed on the basis of specifications issued by the Air Ministry for a ten-passenger high-speed transport.

But the Heinkel never carried any fare-paying passengers.

The prototype "transports" were turned over to the *Luftwaffe* almost immediately and put to work mapping Germany's potential enemies.

The He 111s of the Condor Legion saw their first action in March 1937 over Spain. Experience gained in combat during the Spanish Civil War revealed several shortcomings that were corrected in later production models. One change resulted in an all-new glass nose that substantially increased aircrew visibility.

The He 111s were produced in greater numbers than any other German bomber. The Confederate Air Force He 111 is a German-designed C.A.S.A.

A rare Stinson V-77, best known as the AT-19.

2111 T8 built under license in Spain and powered by two Rolls-Royce 500-29 engines.

In 1937 engineer Jiro Horikoshi was handed the Imperial Japanese Navy's requirements for a fighter with a maximum speed of over 310 miles per hour at 13,000 feet. Japan needed an airplane that could climb to 10,000 feet in three minutes, had an internal fuel endurance of an hour and a half, and could be operated from a carrier deck with an engine in the 1,000-horsepower class.

George "Pappy" Paxton could not believe his eyes one day in 1941 when he and other pilots of Claire Chennault's American Volunteer Group (AVG) Flying Tigers were jumped by a flock of what they thought were Japanese Zeros near Rangoon.

Paxton was thirty-six, not a young twenty-six, when he lied about his age to enlist with the Navy in 1938. When a recruiting officer from Camco

(left) The de Havilland Mosquito used on pathfinder, photo, and night missions could outrun the German Messerschmitt.

A German BF 109 Messerschmitt prowls the sky in search of Allied bombers.

A Sea Fury sporting the Canadian Maple Leaf.

A T-6 modified to represent a Japanese Zero for the "Tora! Tora! Tora!" portion of CAF airshows.

(a New York company acting as agent for the Chinese government) came along with carte-blanche orders from President Roosevelt to recruit any pilot he wanted for duty as a "commercial" pilot in China with the AVG, Paxton decided he'd better sign on before being caught by the Navy.

An automatic honorable discharge was given to any pilot accepting Camco's offer. According to Paxton the officer was having trouble getting fighter pilots, so one night George and four others got him drunk and persuaded him to sign them up.

Chennault knew Paxton had lied about his age. He assigned him additional duty as finance officer but kept him flying. It was just over a year after going to Burma, according to Flying Tigers Panda Bear Squadron Leader David "Tex" Hill, that Paxton took sixty-four Japanese rounds in his P-40B and had to belly-in after the surprise attack.

"We pulled Pappy out of the airplane covered in blood and all he said before passing out was 'I still say the bastards can't shoot.'"

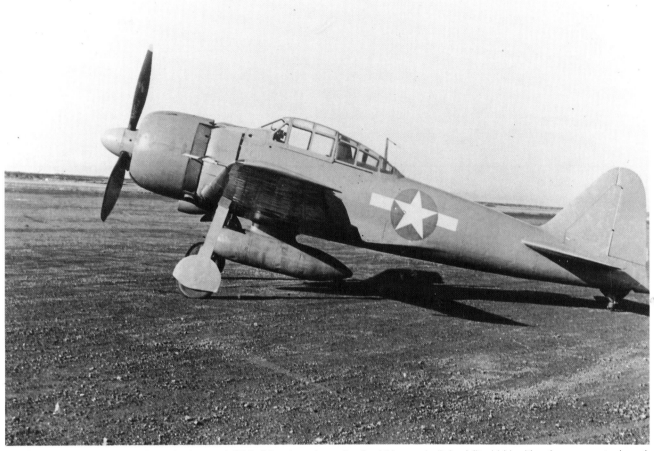

A captured Japanese Navy Zero (nicknamed "Zeke" by American pilots) which was built by Mitsubishi with a long-range tank and American markings.

Paxton had not been shot down by the Zero. The Japanese airplanes over Burma were the Hayabusa, built by the Nakajima company for the Japanese Army. True, the plane was similar. In fact, its engine went to the Japanese Navy's Zero. But the Japanese had carefully managed to place the ultimate fear in the hearts of their enemies for the mysterious Zero.

Paxton steadfastly believed he had been the victim of Horikoshi's Zero, and not the lesser known Hayabusa.

"I wish I had met him so I could tell him what a hell of an airplane he built," Paxton said shortly before his death.

"But I'll never admit those pilots knew how to shoot."

Now they sit side by side on the Confederate Air Force ramp—the restored and flying Japanese Zero and Curtiss P-40 Warhawk. Grey silhouettes alone in the night... ghosts made of metal and memories.

(overleaf) The British Hawker Sea Fury was in production at the end of the war. Powered by a Bristol Centaurus 18 engine, it boasts a five-bladed prop. 173

EPILOGUE

*Wars are fought today not solely by ground,
naval, and air forces but by all citizens united in a joint effort.
The danger zone of modern war is not restricted to battle lines
but extends to the innermost parts of a nation.
No one is immune from the ravages of war.*

As a nation we were not prepared for World War II.
Yes, we won the war, but at a terrific cost of lives,
human suffering, and material.
At times the margin of winning was narrow.
History alone can reveal how many turning points there were,
how many times we were near losing,
and how our enemies' mistakes often pulled us through.
In the flush of victory,
some like to forget these unpalatable truths.

Although we were woefully unprepared as a nation,
we still had the time so essential to build a military force,
time given us by our Allies fighting with their backs to the wall,
and by the distance of oceans.
That precious time will not be given us again.

It is the American people who will decide
whether this nation will continue to hold its air supremacy.
In the final analysis, our air power belongs
to those who come from the ranks of
labor, management, the farms, the stores, the professions,
the schools and colleges and the legislative halls.

Air power will always be
the business of every American citizen.
There will have to be those who refuse to let this fact be forgotten.
Those who will stand up when it would be easier to sit back, those
who will look up when it would be easier to look away.

I may never know their names or see their faces,
but they are not strangers to me.
They are the men and women with the same skills
as those who cut the metal, oiled the engines
and mended the gashes so we could keep winning
a war spread over two oceans.

They are the men and women who understand
that you prepare for peace by keeping prepared for war.
Even now as our forces are being reduced
and we move beyond the smoke of Europe
and the destruction of Japan,
I believe there are those who will rise up
to continue teaching the lessons we have just been taught.

They will ensure that the aviation spirit
born in World War II is never allowed to die.

General Hap Arnold, 1946

Is it true what some claimed?

That on star-filled nights these ghostly galleons of the sky lead an invisible echelon of winged spirits in silent review above the hulk of a once-proud Hellcat rotting in the sands of an Arizona desert?

Or is it merely memory playing tricks on the imaginations of round-engine mechanics who swear these cowlings are warm and the oil is hot even before the first flight of the morning?

Trick or truth, what matters come dawn is that the oily engines fire, the giant props turn . . . .

And the old airplanes fly once again.

PHOTO CREDITS

APPENDIX

Technical specifications are given for American planes mentioned in the text and shown in photographs. Specifications given are greatly simplified and are either those usually regarded as "typical" of the plane or else the latest production run that would have seen service in World War II. For more detailed and complete specifications, see older editions of *Jane's All The World's Aircraft* or one of Bill Gunston's fine reference books.

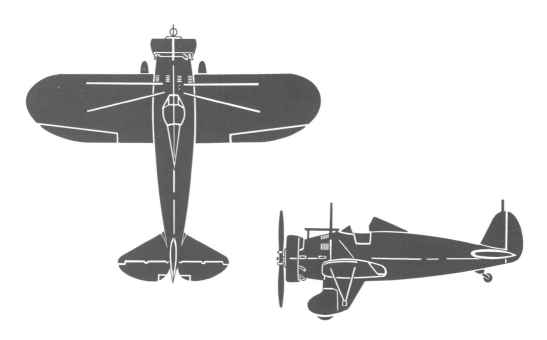

P-26 (Boeing)

Type: single-seat pursuit fighter

Engine: one 600-hp Pratt & Whitney nine-cylinder radial

Dimensions: 27-ft., 11.5-in. wing span, length 23 ft. 9 in.

Weights: empty 2,200 lb., loaded 3,075 lb.

Speed and Range: maximum speed 235 mph, range (loaded) 635 mi., with a ceiling of 28,000 ft.

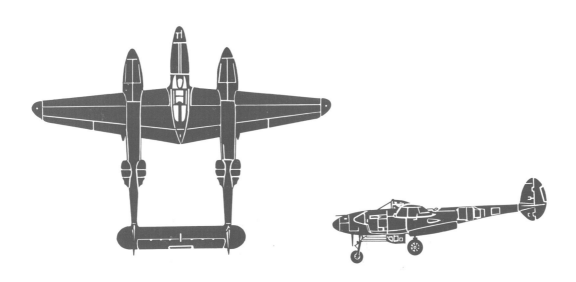

P-38 Lightning (Lockheed)

Type: single-seat long-range fighter

Engines: two 1,600-hp Allison liquid-cooled

Dimensions: 52-ft. wing span, length 37 ft. 10 in.

Weights: empty 12,700 lb., loaded 21,600-lb. maximum

Speed and Range: maximum speed 414 mph, range (loaded) 2,260 mi., with a ceiling of 30,000 ft.

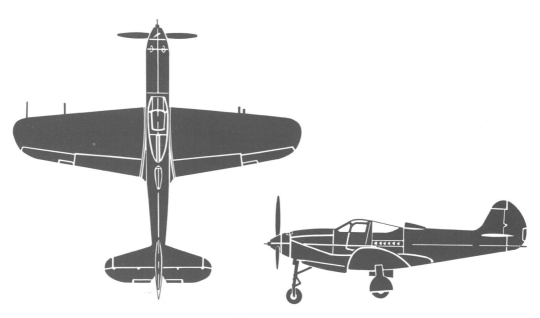

P-39 Airacobra (Bell)

Type: single-seat fighter

Engine: one 1,325-hp Allison liquid-cooled

Dimensions: 34-ft. wing span, length 30 ft. 2 in.

Weights: empty 5,600 lb., loaded 7,780 lb.

Speed and Range: maximum speed 380 mph, range (loaded) 1,475 mi., with a ceiling of 35,000 ft.

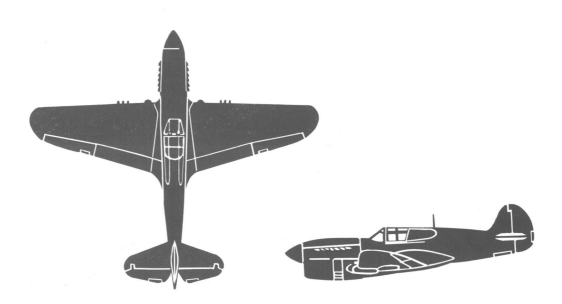

P-40 Warhawk (Curtiss)

Type: single-seat fighter

Engine: one 1,040-hp Allison liquid-cooled on the P-40C Tomahawk IIB, and one 1,300-hp Packard liquid-cooled on the P-40F Kittyhawk II

Dimensions: 37-ft., 3.5-in. wing span, length (P-40C) 31 ft. 8.5 in., (P-40F) 31 ft. 2 in.

Weights: empty (P-40C) 5,812 lb., (P-40F) 6,550 lb., loaded (P-40C) 7,459 lb., (P-40F) 8,720 lb.

Speed and Range: maximum speed (P-40C) 345 mph, (P-40F) 364 mph, range (P-40C) 730 mi., (P-40F) 610 mi., with a ceiling of 30,000 ft.

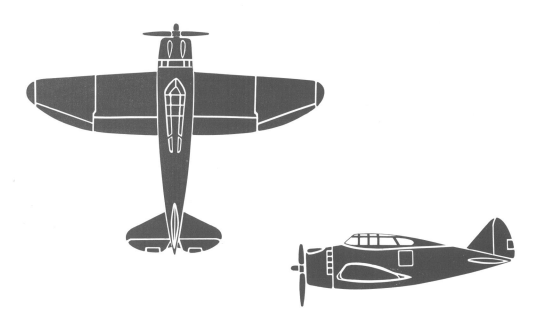

P-43 Lancer (Republic)

Type: single-seat fighter

Engine: one 1200-hp Pratt & Whitney R-1830

Dimensions: 36-ft. wing span, length 28 ft. 6 in.

Weights: empty 5,654 lb., loaded 7,810 lb.

Speed and Range: maximum speed 350 mph, range 1,300 mi., with a ceiling of 38,000 ft.

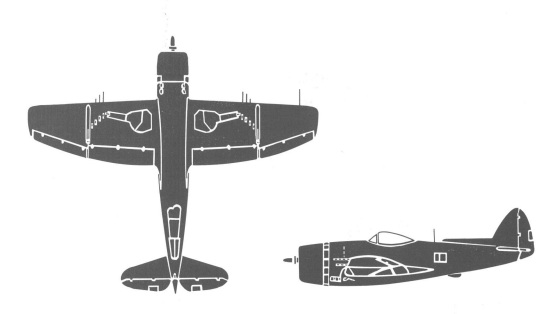

P-47 Thunderbolt (Republic)

Type: single-seat fighter, fighter-bomber

Engine: one 2,300-hp Pratt & Whitney Double Wasp 18-cylinder two-row radial

Dimensions: 40-ft., 9.25-in. wing span, length 36 ft. 1.25 in.

Weights: empty 10,700 lb., loaded 19,400 lb.

Speed and Range: maximum speed 428 mph, range (loaded) 1,900 mi., with a ceiling of 43,000 ft.

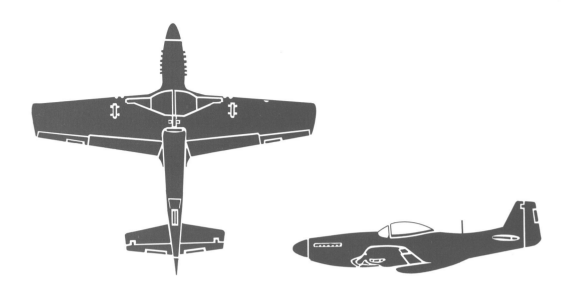

P-51 Mustang (North American)

Type: single-seat fighter

Engine: one 1,150-hp Allison liquid-cooled; later versions used Packard, Rolls Royce, and Lycoming engines

Dimensions: 37-ft., 0.5-in. wing span, length 33 ft. 4 in.

Weights: empty (P-51D) 7,125 lb., loaded (P-51D) 11,600 lb.

Speed and Range: maximum speed (P-51D) 437 mph, range (P-51D) 1,300 mi., with a ceiling of 41,900 ft.

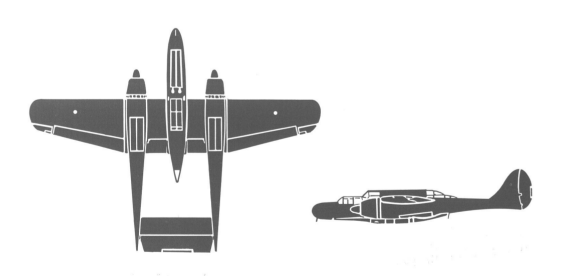

P-61 Black Widow (Northrop)

Type: three-seat night fighter

Engines: two 2,000-hp Pratt & Whitney 18-cylinder two-row radials

Dimensions: 66-ft. wing span, length 49 ft. 7 in.

Weights: empty 24,000 lb., loaded 40,300 lb.

Speed and Range: maximum speed 430 mph, range (loaded) 2,800 mi., with a ceiling of 41,000 ft.

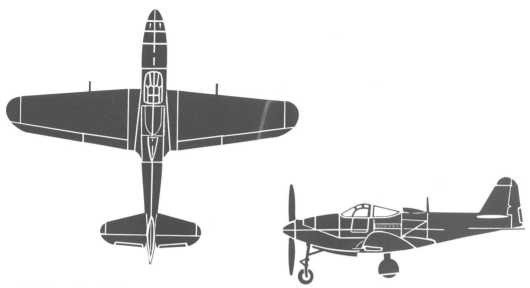

P-63 Kingcobra (Bell)

Type: single-seat fighter

Engine: 1,100-hp Allison

Dimensions: 38-ft., 4-in. wing span, length 32 ft. 8 in.

Weights: empty 6,800 lb., loaded 10,700 lb.

Speed and Range: maximum speed 410 mph, range 320 mi., with a ceiling of 25,000 ft.

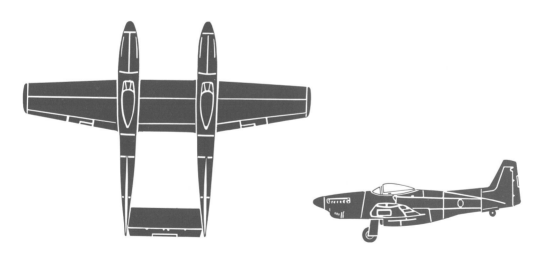

P-82 Twin Mustang (North American)

Type: twin-fuselage, single-seat night fighter

Engines: two 2,300-hp Allison

Dimensions: 51-ft., 3-in. wing span, length 42 ft. 2 in.

Weights: empty 14,350 lb., loaded 26,208 lb.

Speed and Range: maximum speed 465 mph, range (loaded) 2,200 mi., with a ceiling of 41,900 ft.

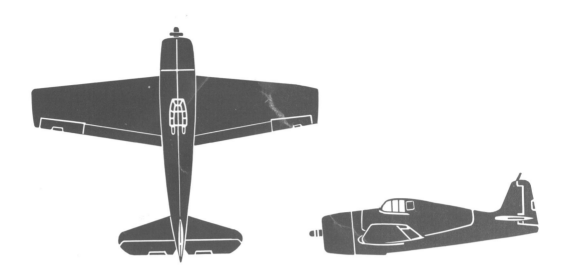

F6F Hellcat (Grumman)

Type: single-seat carrier-based naval fighter

Engine: one 2000-hp Pratt & Whitney R-2800

Dimensions: 42-ft., 10-in. wing span, length 33 ft.

Weights: empty 9,101 lb., loaded 12,441 lb.

Speed and Range: maximum speed 375 mph, range 1,590 mi., with a ceiling of 37,300 ft.

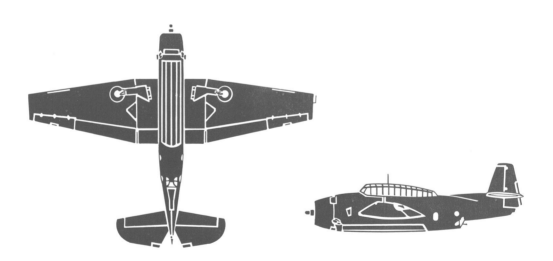

TBM Avenger (Eastern), **TBF** Avenger (Grumman)

Type: three-seat torpedo-bomber

Engine: one 1,700-hp Wright 14-cylinder

Dimensions: 54-ft., 2-in. wing span, length 48 ft. ⅛ in.

Weights: loaded 15,536 lb.

Speed and Range: maximum speed 278 mph, range (loaded) 905 mi., with a ceiling of 22,600 ft.

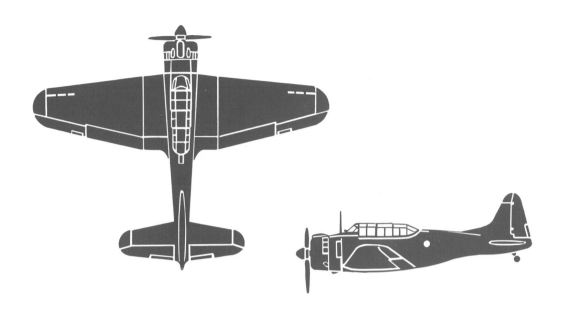

SBD Dauntless (Douglas)

Type: two-seat carrier-based scout plane and dive-bomber

Engine: one 1,000-hp Wright Cyclone R-1820

Dimensions: 41-ft., 6-in. wing span, length 32 ft. 8 in.

Weights: empty 6,345 lb., loaded 9,407 lb.

Speed and Range: maximum speed 250 mph, range (loaded) 1,200 mi., (scout) 1,400-1,500 mi., with a ceiling of 27,100 ft.

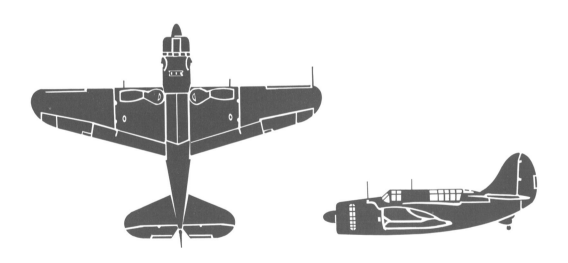

SB2C Helldiver (Curtiss)

Type: two-seat carrier-based scout plane and dive-bomber

Engine: one 1900-hp Wright R-2600

Dimensions: 49-ft., 9-in. wing span, length 36 ft. 8 in.

Weights: empty 10,547 lb., loaded 14,189 lb.

Speed and Range: maximum speed 295 mph, range (loaded) 1,165 mi., (scout) 1,235 mi., with a ceiling of 29,100 ft.

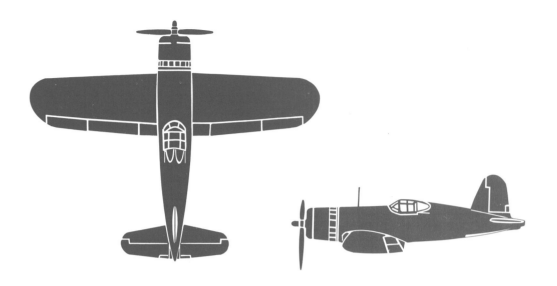

F4U Corsair (Vought)

Type: single-seat carrier-based fighter-bomber

Engine: one 2,000-hp Pratt & Whitney Double Wasp 18-cylinder two-row radial

Dimensions: 40-ft., 11.75-in. wing span, length 33 ft. 8.25 in.

Weights: empty 8,873 lb., loaded 14,000 lb.

Speed and Range: maximum speed 395 mph, range (loaded) 1,000 mi., with a ceiling of 44,000 ft.

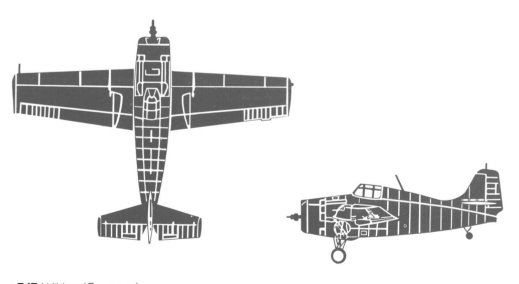

F4F Wildcat (Grumman)

Type: single-engine naval fighter

Engine: one 1,050-hp Pratt & Whitney 14-cylinder two-row radial

Dimensions: 34-ft., 6-in. wing span, length 24 ft. 6 in.

Weights: empty 3,300 lb., loaded 4,828 lb.

Speed and Range: maximum speed 325 mph, range (loaded) 920 mi., with a ceiling of 34,000 ft.

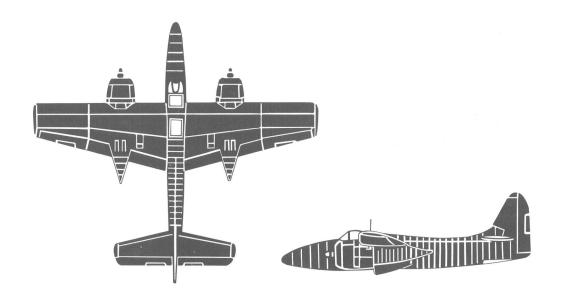

F7F Tigercat (Grumman)

Type: single- or two-seat fighter-bomber or night fighter
Engines: two 2,100-hp Pratt & Whitney Double Wasp 18-cylinder two-row radials
Dimensions: 51-ft., 6-in. wing span, length 45 ft. 4 in.
Weights: empty 13,100 lb., loaded 22,560 lb.
Speed and Range: maximum speed 427 mph, range 1,170 mi., with a ceiling of 40,700 ft.

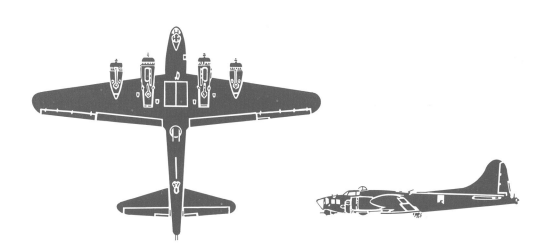

B-17 Flying Fortress (Boeing)

Type: high-altitude bomber with crew of six to ten
Engines: four 1,200-hp Wright Cyclone nine-cylinder
Dimensions: 103-ft., 9-in. wing span, length 74 ft. 9 in.
Weights: empty 35,800 lb., loaded 46,650 lb.
Speed and Range: maximum speed 287 mph, range (loaded) 1,100 mi., with a ceiling of 35,000 ft.

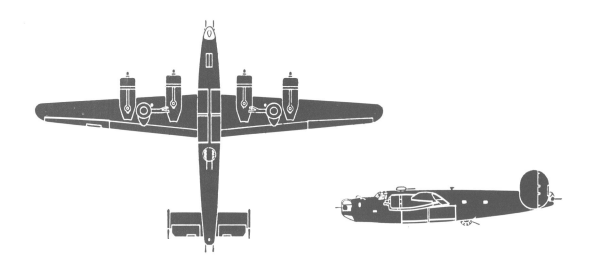

B-24 Liberator (Consolidated Vultee)

Type: long-range bomber with normal crew of 10
Engines: four 1,200-hp Pratt & Whitney 14-cylinder two-row radials
Dimensions: 110-ft. wing span, length 67 ft. 2 in.
Weights: empty 37,000 lb., loaded 65,000 lb.
Speed and Range: maximum speed 290 mph, range (loaded) 2,200 mi., with a ceiling of 28,000 ft.

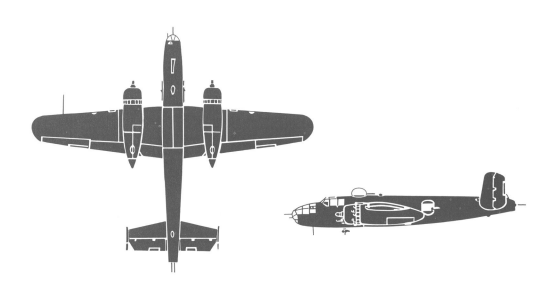

B-25 Mitchell (North American)

Type: medium bomber or attack crew of four to six
Engines: two 1,700-hp Wright 14-cylinder two-row radials
Dimensions: 67-ft., 7-in. wing span, length 54 ft. 1 in.
Weights: empty 21,100 lb., loaded 35,000 lb.
Speed and Range: maximum speed 315 mph, range (loaded) 1,500 mi., with a ceiling of 24,000 ft.

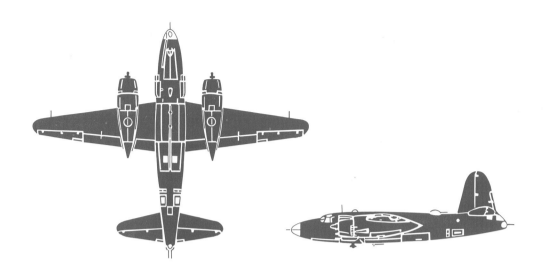

B-26 Marauder (Martin)

Type: five- to seven-seat medium bomber
Engines: two Pratt & Whitney 18-cylinder two-row radials
Dimensions: 71-ft. wing span, length 56 ft. 6 in.
Weights: empty 25,300 lb., loaded 37,000 lb.
Speed and Range: maximum speed 310 mph, range (loaded) 1,150 mi., with a ceiling of 19,800 ft.

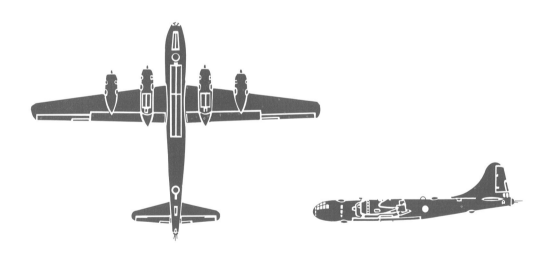

B-29 Superfortress (Boeing)

Type: high-altitude heavy bomber with crew of ten to fourteen
Engines: four 2,200-hp Wright Cyclone 18-cylinder
Dimensions: 141-ft., 3-in. wing span, length 99 ft.
Weights: empty 74,500 lb., loaded 147,000 lb.
Speed and Range: speed 325 mph, range (loaded) 3,700 mi., with a ceiling of 33,000 ft.

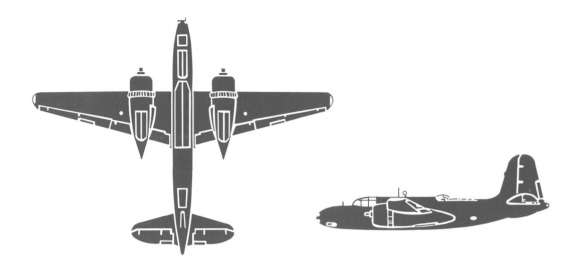

A-20 Havoc (Douglas)

Type: two-seat fighter, three-seat bomber, or two-seat reconnaissance plane

Engines: two 1,200-hp Pratt & Whitney; later versions, two 1,500-, 1,600-, or 1,700-hp Wright engines

Dimensions: 61-ft., 4-in. wing span, length varied from 45 ft., 11 in. to 48 ft., 10 in.

Weights: early versions: empty 11,400 lb., loaded 16,700 lb.; later versions (A20G, e.g.) empty 12,950 lb., loaded 27,200 lb.

Speed and Range: maximum speed later versions, 351 mph; range (loaded) 1,000 mi., with a maximum ceiling of 25,300 ft.

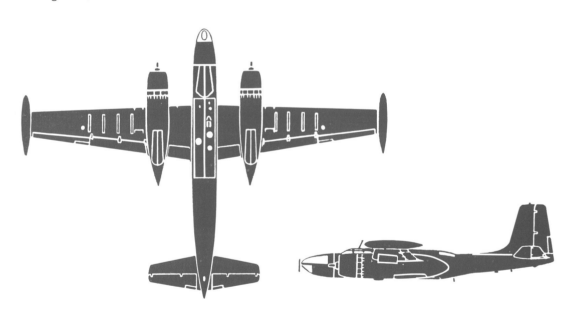

A-26 Invader (Douglas)

Type: three-seat attack bomber

Engines: two 2,000-hp Pratt & Whitney

Dimensions: 70-ft. wing span, length 50 ft.

Weights: empty 22,370 lb., loaded 27,000 lb.; later, 35,000 lb.

Speed and Range: maximum speed 355 mph; range (loaded) 1,400 mi., with a maximum ceiling of 22,100 ft.

C-46 Commando (Curtiss)

Type: troop or cargo transport
Engines: two 2,000-hp Pratt & Whitney Double Wasp 18-cylinder
Dimensions: 108-ft., 1-in. wing span, length 76 ft. 4 in.
Weights: empty 29,483 lb., loaded 45,000 lb.
Speed and Range: maximum speed 265 mph, range n/a, with a ceiling of 24,500 ft.

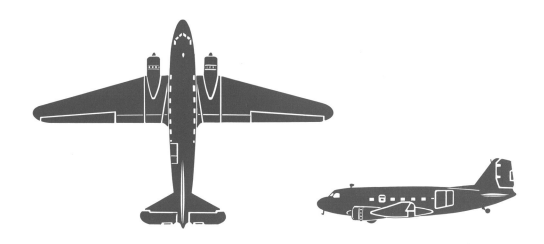

C-47 Skytrain (Douglas)

Type: utility, troop transport
Engines: two 12,00-hp Pratt & Whitney 14-cylinder, two-row radials
Dimensions: 95-ft. wing span, length 64 ft. 5.5 in.
Weights: empty 16,970 lb., loaded 25,200 lb.
Speed and Range: maximum speed 230 mph, range (loaded) 2,125 mi., with a ceiling of 23,000 ft.

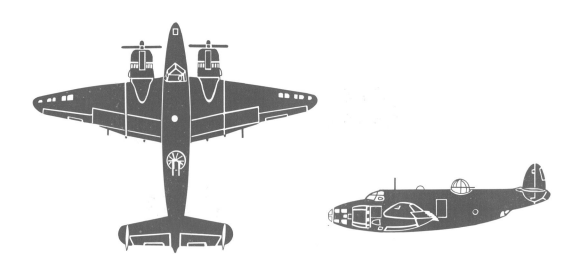

PV-2 Harpoon (Lockheed-Vega)

Type: over-water patrol

Engines: two 1,600-hp Pratt & Whitney

Dimensions: 75-ft. wing span, length 52 ft. 1 in.

Weights: empty 21,028 lb., loaded 36,000 lb.

Speed and Range: maximum speed 282 mph, range (loaded) 1,790 mi., with a ceiling of 23,900 ft.

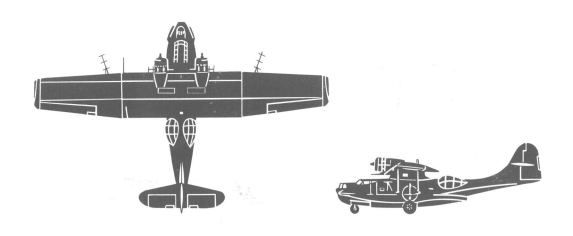

PBY Catalina (Consolidated Vultee)

Type: maritime patrol boat with normal crew of seven

Engines: two 1,200-hp Pratt & Whitney Twin Wasp 14-cylinder two-row radials

Dimensions: 104-ft. wing span, length 63 ft. 11 in.

Weights: empty 17,465 lb., loaded 34,000 lb.

Speed and Range: maximum speed 196 mph, range (loaded) 3,100 mi., with a ceiling of 18,200 ft.

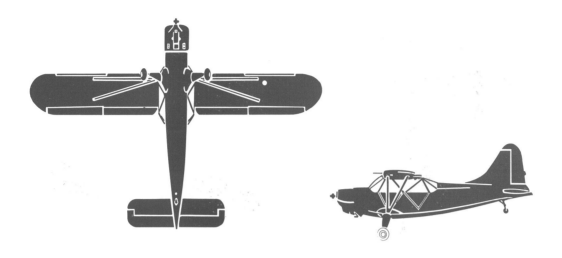

L-5 Sentinel (Stinson)

Type: two-seat liaison/observation or ambulance plane
Engine: one 190-hp Lycoming six-cylinder
Dimensions: 34-ft. wing span, length 24 ft. 1.25 in.
Weights: empty 1,472 lb., loaded 2,158 lb.
Speed and Range: maximum speed 129 mph, range n/a, with a ceiling of 15,800 ft.

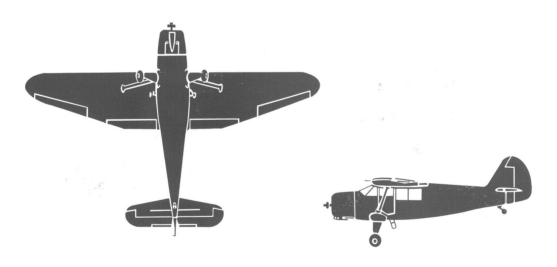

AT-19 Reliant (Stinson)

Type: three-seat navigational trainer
Engine: one 290-hp Lycoming nine-cylinder radial
Dimensions: 41-ft. 10.5-in. wing span, length 29 ft. 4.25 in.
Weights: empty 2,810 lb., loaded 4,000 lb.
Speed and Range: maximum speed 141 mph, range n/a, with a ceiling of 14,000 ft.

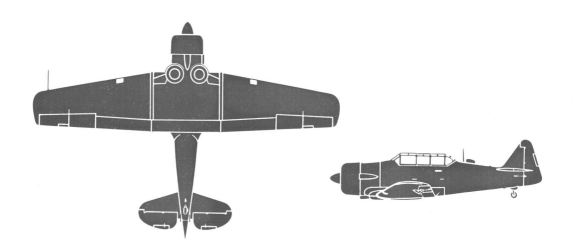

AT-6/SNJ Texan (North American)

Type: two-seat (some single) trainer and light attack
Engine: one 600-hp Pratt & Whitney
Dimensions: 41-ft. wing span, length 29 ft. 6 in.
Weights: empty 4,271 lb., loaded 5,617 lb.
Speed and Range: maximum speed 212 mph; range 870 mi., with a ceiling of 22,750 ft.

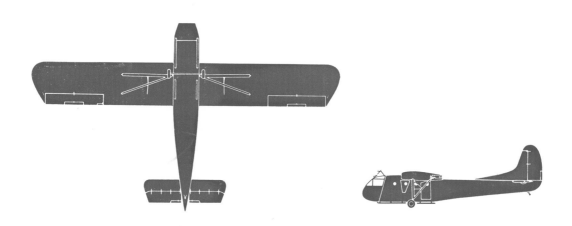

CG-4A Haig (Waco)

Type: assault glider
Engine: none
Dimensions: 83-ft., 8-in. wing span, length 39 ft. 9 in.
Weights: empty 3,790 lb., loaded 7,500 lb.
Speed and Range: off-tow 55 mph, minimum speed 38 mph.